D1527814

# FLORIDA AND ARKANSAS

COMPENDIUM OF THE CONFEDERATE ARMIES

# FLORIDA AND ARKANSAS

*Stewart Sifakis*

 Facts On File
*New York • Oxford*

## COMPENDIUM OF THE CONFEDERATE ARMIES: FLORIDA AND ARKANSAS

Copyright © 1992 by Stewart Sifakis

Facts On File, Inc.          Facts On File Limited
460 Park Avenue South    Collins Street
New York NY 10016        Oxford OX4 1XJ
USA                               United Kingdom

**Library of Congress Cataloging-in-Publication Data**

Sifakis, Stewart.
  Compendium of the Confederate armies / Stewart Sifakis.
     p.  cm.
  Includes bibliographical references and indexes.
  Contents: Virginia — Tennessee — Alabama —
Florida and Arkansas — North Carolina.
  ISBN 0-8160-2288-7
  1. Confederate States of America. Army—History.  2. United
States—History—Civil War. 1861–1865—Regimental histories.
I. Title.
E546.S58   1991
973.7'42—dc20                                                                   90-23631

A British CIP catalogue record for this book is available from the British Library.

Text design by Ron Monteleone
Composition by Facts On File, Inc.
Manufactured by the Maple-Vail Book Manufacturing Group
Printed in the United States of America

10 9 8 7 6 5 4 3 2 1

This book is printed on acid-free paper.

*To*
*The Memory of James Sifakis*
*1893–1961*

# CONTENTS

# ACKNOWLEDGMENTS

I am deeply indebted for this work to the personnel, past and present, of Facts On File, especially to Edward Knappman, Gerry Helferich, and my editors: Kate Kelly, Helen Flynn, Eleanora Von Dehsen, Traci Cothran and Nicholas Bakalar. Also I would like to thank the staffs of the National Archives, Library of Congress, the various state archives and the New York Public Library for their patience and assistance. Over the past decades the staff of the National Park Service, Edwin C. Bearss, chief historian, have proven very informative on my frequent visits to the various battlefields. To Shaun Potter, Christina Villano and Sally Gadsby I am indebted for keeping me at my work. For the logistical support of the management of the Hotel Post, Zermatt (Karl Ivarsson, Ursula Waeny and Leslie Dawkins), I am very grateful. And last, but certainly not least, I owe thanks to John Warren for his knowledge of computers, without which this project would have ground to a halt, and to his computer widow, Evelyne.

# INTRODUCTION

This work is intended to be the companion set to Frederick H. Dyer's *Compendium of the War of the Rebellion* for the Confederacy. The compendium was first published as a three-volume work in 1909. A study of all the Union regiments, battalions, batteries and independent companies, it has since been reprinted in two- and one-volume editions.

It has been estimated that for every day since the end of the American Civil War, one book, magazine or newspaper article has appeared dealing with some aspect of that fratricidal struggle. Many ask: If so much has been written on the Civil War, is there really a need for more? The answer is an emphatic yes. Many aspects of the conflict have been covered only superficially and require much more in-depth research. But for such research a bedrock of reference works is essential.

There are many such works available, including the U.S. War Department's 128-volume *The War of the Rebellion: A Compilation of the Official Records of the Union and Confederate Armies* and the U.S. Navy Department's 31-volume *Official Records of the Union and Confederate Navies in the War of the Rebellion.* Registers of military personnel include: George W. Cullum's two-volume *Biographical Register of the Officers and Graduates of the United States Military Academy,* Francis B. Heitman's two-volume *Historical Register and Dictionary of the United States Army From Its Organization, September 29, 1789, to March 2, 1903,* Guy V. Henry's two-volume *Military Record of Civilian Appointments in the United States Army,* Robert K. Krick's *Lee's Colonels: A Biographical Register of the Field Officers of the Army of Northern Virginia* and Ezra J. Warner's *Generals in Gray: Lives of the Confederate Commanders* and *Generals in Blue: Lives of the Union Commanders.* Politics are covered in Jon L. Wakelyn's *Biographical Dictionary of the Confederacy* and Ezra J. Warner's and W. Buck Yearns' *Biographical Register of the Confederate Congress.* E. B. Long's *The Civil War Day by Day: An Almanac 1861-1865* provides an excellent chronology. Collective biographies include Mark M. Boatner's *The Civil War Dictionary,* Patricia L. Faust's *Historical Times Illustrated Encyclopedia of the Civil War* and Stewart

Sifakis' *Who Was Who in the Civil War*. Then, of course there is Dyer's compendium.

To date there has not been a comprehensive equivalent to Dyer's work for the South as a whole. Basically work has been done by individual states. North Carolina has an excellent work currently nearing completion. Other commendable works have been done for Tennessee, Virginia and Texas. Works were begun for Georgia and South Carolina but did not proceed far. State government agencies in Florida and Kentucky made some efforts in the early years after the war. However, none of these draws a consolidated picture of the Confederate States Army. That is where the *Compendium of the Confederate Armies* comes in.

This work is organized into volumes by state. One volume includes the border state units—Kentucky, Maryland and Missouri, units organized directly by the Confederate authorities from various state companies and those units from the Indian nations allied with the Confederacy. The final volume consists of the tables of organization of the various armies and departments throughout the war.

There are chapters in each volume on the artillery, cavalry and infantry. Those units having a numerical designation are listed first, followed by those units using the name of their commander, home region or some other name. Units are then broken down alphabetically by size—battalions, batteries, companies and regiments. If two or more units still have the same sorting features, they are then further broken down alphabetically by any special designation—1st or 2nd Organization, Local Defense Troops, Militia, Provisional Army, Regulars, Reserves, Sharpshooters, State Guard, State Line, State Troops or Volunteers. The company designation for artillery batteries that served within an artillery battalion or regiment is listed at the end of the battalion or regiment designation. If heavy artillery battalions or regiments served together as a unit through most of the war, they are treated as a whole with no breakdown of the companies.

Each entry starts with the unit's name. Any nicknames or other mistaken designations follow. Then comes a summary of its organizational details: its date and location of organization, mustering into service, the number of companies for battalion organizations, armament for artillery batteries, surrenders, paroles, exchanges and disbandment or mustering out. The next paragraph starts with the first commanding officer and continues with an alphabetical listing of the other field-grade officers. (Captains are listed chronologically for artillery batteries.) The next paragraph is the brigade and higher-level command assignments of the unit. This is followed by a listing of the battles and campaigns the unit was engaged in. Note that the unit was not necessarily present on each date that is indicated for multiday actions. The final paragraph is the suggested further reading, if any.

Because records are incomplete, I have dropped the list of casualties of each unit that Dyer includes for the Northern units. But I have added to Dyer's format by including the first commanding officer and the field-grade officers of each unit. Selected bibliographies are included for each volume. Also, as available, unit histories and personal memoirs are listed with some units as suggested further reading.

# FLORIDA

# FLORIDA UNITS

Florida seceded from the Union on January 10, 1861. Upon the creation of the Confederate army, Florida's forces were incorporated into it.

One specialized type of unit was organized for the army: the Reserves, created by the Confederate Congress on February 17, 1864, when it expanded conscription to include all white males between 17 and 50 years of age. Those under 18 and those over 45 were to be organized in the Reserves, troops that did not have to serve beyond the boundaries of the state.

In general, the units that remained within the state's boundaries were generally independent companies and battalions serving in small detachments throughout the sparsely populated region. They were organized into regiments only when they were about to be sent to the fronts in Virginia and Tennessee.

Note: The index for the Florida units begins on page 139.

# ARTILLERY

### 1. FLORIDA COAST GUARD ARTILLERY
*Organization:* Organized in 1861. Served aboard the *General Grayson* for a time. Apparently mustered out in May 1862.
*First Commander:* Simmons (Captain)
*Assignment:* Department of Middle and Eastern Florida (December 1861-May 1862)

### 2. FLORIDA GRAYSON ARTILLERY
*Organization:* Organized in 1861. Apparently mustered out in May 1862.
*First Commander:* H. T. Baya (Captain)
*Assignment:* Department of Middle and Eastern Florida (December 1861-May 1862)

### 3. FLORIDA KILCREASE ARTILLERY
*Organization:* Organized on May 27, 1863, by the division of the Leon Artillery by order of Major General Howell Cobb, commanding District of Middle Florida, dated May 25, 1863. Initial armament comprised four 3.5-inch Blakely Rifles. Armed from May 1863 to January 1865 with two 12-lb. Howitzers and two 6-lb. Smoothbores. Surrendered at Tallahassee, Florida, by Major General Samuel Jones, commanding the District of Florida on May 10, 1865.
*First Commander:* F. L. Villepique (Captain)
*Captain:* P. Houston
*Assignments:* District of Middle Florida, Department of South Carolina, Georgia and Florida (May-August 1863)
District of Georgia, Department of South Carolina, Georgia and Florida (August-November or December 1863)
2nd Military District of South Carolina, Department of South Carolina, Georgia and Florida (November or December 1863-February 1864)

Light Artillery, District of Florida, Department of South Carolina, Georgia and
Florida (February-July 1864)

Jackson's-Miller's Brigade (District of Florida), Department of South Carolina,
Georgia and Florida (July-December 1864)

8th Light Artillery Battalion, Miller's-Jones' Brigade (District of Florida), Department of South Carolina, Georgia and Florida (December 1864-May 1865)

## 4. FLORIDA LEON ARTILLERY

*Nickname:* Florida Light Artillery

*Organization:* Organized for the war on March 3, 1862. Converted to heavy
artillery service in early 1864. Armed from May 1864 to January 1865 with two
3-inch Rifles and two 12-lb. Howitzers. Surrendered at Tallahassee, Florida, by
Major General Samuel Jones, commanding the District of Florida, on May 10,
1865.

*First Commander:* Robert H. Gamble (Captain)

*Captain:* Charles E. Dyke

*Assignments:* Department of Middle and Eastern Florida (March-October
1862)

District of East and Middle Florida, Department of South Carolina, Georgia
and Florida (October-November 1862)

District of Middle Florida, Department of South Carolina, Georgia and Florida
(November 1862-February 1864)

Unattached, District of East Florida, Department of South Carolina, Georgia
and Florida (February 1864)

Light Artillery, District of Florida, Department of South Carolina, Georgia and
Florida (February-July 1864)

Jackson's-Miller's Brigade (District of Florida), Department of South Carolina,
Georgia and Florida (July-December 1864)

8th Light Artillery Battalion, Miller's-Jones' Brigade (District of Florida), Department of South Carolina, Georgia and Florida (December 1864-May 1865)

*Battles:* St. John's Island, Florida (September 11, 1862)

near Jacksonville (March 25, 1863)

Olustee (February 20, 1864)

## 5. FLORIDA MARION ARTILLERY

*Organization:* Organized for 12 months on December 12, 1861. Reorganized
for two years or the war on May 12, 1862. Armed between December 1863 and
March 1864 with two 12-lb. Howitzers and two 6-lb. Smoothbores. Armed in
April 1864 with four 12-lb. Smoothbores. Surrendered by Lieutenant General
Richard Taylor at Citronelle, Alabama, on May 4, 1865.

*First Commander:* John M. Martin (Captain)

*Captains:* Robert P. McCants

Thomas J. Perry

*Assignments:* Department of Middle and Eastern Florida (December 1861-February 1862)

Army of Pensacola, Department of Alabama and West Florida (February-February or March 1862)

Department of Middle and Eastern Florida (February or March-May 1862)

Davis' Brigade, Heth's Division, Department of East Tennessee (July-December 1862)

Unattached, Department of East Tennessee (December 1862-February or March 1863)

A. E. Jackson's Brigade, Department of East Tennessee (February or March-March or April 1863)

Davis'-Maxwell's-Trigg's Brigade, Department of East Tennessee (March or April-September 1863)

Reserve Artillery, Buckner's Corps, Army of Tennessee (September-September or October 1863)

Williams' Battalion, Artillery, 1st Corps, Army of Tennessee (September or October-November 1863)

Williams' Battalion, Reserve Artillery, Army of Tennessee (November-November or December 1863)

Smith's-Hoxton's Artillery Battalion, Cheatham's Division, 1st Corps, Army of Tennessee (November or December 1863-February 1864)

Hoxton's Battalion, Artillery, 1st Corps, Army of Tennessee (February 1864-January 1865)

Gee's Artillery Battalion, Right Wing, Defenses of Mobile, Artillery Reserves, etc., District of the Gulf, Department of Alabama, Mississippi and East Louisiana (March-April 1865)

3rd Battalion, Smith's Brigade, Department of Alabama, Mississippi and East Louisiana (April-May 1865)

*Battles:* Richmond, Kentucky (August 30, 1862)

Chickamauga (September 19-20, 1863)

Chattanooga Siege (September-November 1863)

Chattanooga (November 23-25, 1863)

Atlanta Campaign (May-September 1864)

Atlanta Siege (July-September 1864)

Nashville (December 15-16, 1864)

Mobile (March 17-April 12, 1865)

## 6. FLORIDA MILTON LIGHT ARTILLERY, BATTERY A, ARTILLERY

*Organization:* Organized on March 10, 1862. Armed in May 1864 with two 6-lb. James Rifles, one 12-lb. Napoleon and one 12-lb. Howitzer. In January

1865 armament comprised four 12-lb. Napoleons. Surrendered at Tallahassee, Florida, by Major General Samuel Jones, commanding the District of Florida, on May 10, 1865.

**First Commander:** Joseph L. Dunham (Captain)

**Assignments:** Department of Middle and Eastern Florida (March-October 1862)

District of East and Middle Florida, Department of South Carolina, Georgia and Florida (October-November 1862)

District of Florida, Department of South Carolina, Georgia and Florida (November 1862-February 1864)

Light Artillery, District of Florida, Department of South Carolina, Georgia and Florida (February-July 1864)

Jackson's-Miller's Brigade (District of Florida), Department of South Carolina, Georgia and Florida (July-December 1864)

8th Light Artillery Battalion, Miller's-Jones' Brigade (District of Florida), Department of South Carolina, Georgia and Florida (December 1864-May 1865)

**Battles:** Capture of the USS *Columbine* (May 23, 1864)

St. John's Bluff (September 11, 1862)


## 7. FLORIDA MILTON LIGHT ARTILLERY, BATTERY B, ARTILLERY

**Organization:** Organized by the division of A, Milton Light Artillery, on March 5, 1863. Armed in May 1864 with two 12-lb. Napoleons and two 6-lb. Smoothbores. Armament in December 1864 and January 1865 comprised two 12-lb. Napoleons and two 12-lb. Howitzers. Surrendered at Durham Station, Orange County, North Carolina, on April 26, 1865.

**First Commander:** Henry F. Abell (Captain)

**Assignments:** District of East Florida, Department of South Carolina, Georgia and Florida (March 1863-February 1864)

Light Artillery, District of Florida, Department of South Carolina, Georgia and Florida (February-July 1864)

Jackson's-Miller's Brigade (District of Florida), Department of South Carolina, Georgia and Florida (July-December 1864)

6th (Brooks') Light Artillery Battalion, McLaws' Division, Department of South Carolina, Georgia and Florida (December 1864-April 1865)

Palmer's Artillery Battalion, Unattached, Army of Tennessee (April 1865)

**Battles:** Savannah Campaign (November-December 1864)

Carolinas Campaign (February-April 1865)


## 8. FLORIDA ROBERTSON'S BATTERY

**See:** ALABAMA (AND FLORIDA) ROBERTSON'S-DENT'S ARTILLERY BATTERY

# CAVALRY

## 9. FLORIDA 1ST CAVALRY BATTALION

*Organization:* Organized with eight companies on November 4, 1861. Increased to a regiment and designated as the 1st Cavalry Regiment on January 1, 1862.
*First Commander:* William G. M. Davis (Lieutenant Colonel)
*Field Officer:* William T. Stockton (Major)
*Assignment:* Department of Middle and Eastern Florida (November 1861-January 1862)

## 10. FLORIDA 1ST SPECIAL CAVALRY BATTALION

*Nickname:* Cattle Guards
Special Commissary Battalion
*Organization:* Organized on December 23, 1864. Surrendered at Tallahassee, Florida, by Major General Samuel Jones, commanding the District of Florida, on May 10, 1865.
*First Commander:* Charles J. Munnerlyn (Lieutenant Colonel)
*Field Officer:* William Footman (Major)
*Assignment:* Miller's-Jones' Brigade (District of Florida), Department of South Carolina, Georgia and Florida (December 1864-May 1865)

## 11. FLORIDA 1ST CAVALRY REGIMENT

*Organization:* Organized by the addition of two companies to the 1st Cavalry Battalion on January 1, 1862. Companies had been mustered into Confederate service for 12 months between October 12, 1861, and January 1, 1862. Except for Companies A, E and F, regiment dismounted in the spring of 1862 and served the balance of the war as infantry. Field consolidation with the 4th Infantry Regiment from December 1863 to April 1865. Companies A, E and F dismounted and rejoined the regiment in 1864. Consolidated with the 1st (Reorganized), 3rd, 4th, 6th and 7th Infantry Regiments at Smithfield, North

Carolina, and designated as the 1st Infantry Regiment Consolidated on April 9, 1865.

**First Commander:** William G. M. Davis (Colonel)
**Field Officers:** G. Troup Maxwell (Lieutenant Colonel, Major)
William T. Stockton (Major, Lieutenant Colonel)
**Assignments:** Department of Middle and Eastern Florida (January-March 1862)
Leadbetter's Brigade, Department of East Tennessee (May-June 1862)
Post of Chattanooga, Department of East Tennessee (June-July 1862)
Davis' Brigade, Heth's Division, Department of East Tennessee (July-December 1862)
Davis'-Jackson's-Maxwell's-Trigg's Brigade, Department of East Tennessee (December 1862-September 1863)
Trigg's Brigade, Preston's Division, Buckner's Corps, Army of Tennessee (September-October 1863)
Trigg's Brigade, Buckner's Division, 1st Corps, Army of Tennessee (October-November 1863)
Florida Brigade, Bate's Division, 2nd Corps, Army of Tennessee (November 1863-February 1864)
Florida Brigade, Bate's Division, 1st Corps, Army of Tennessee (February 1864-April 1865)
**Battles:** near Fernandina, Florida (Company F) (April 10, 1862)
Richmond, Kentucky (Companies A, E and F) (August 30, 1862)
Perryville (Companies B, C, D, G, H, I and K) (October 8, 1862)
Chickamauga (September 19-20, 1863)
Chattanooga Siege (September-November 1863)
Chattanooga (November 23-25, 1863)
Atlanta Campaign (May-September 1864)
New Hope Church (May 25-June 5, 1864)
Atlanta (July 22, 1864)
Ezra Church (July 28, 1864)
Atlanta Siege (July-September 1864)
Jonesboro (August 31-September 1, 1864)
Franklin (November 30, 1864)
Nashville (December 15-16, 1864)
Carolinas Campaign (February-April 1865)

## 12. FLORIDA 2ND CAVALRY

**Organization:** Organized from independent companies on December 4, 1862. Surrendered at Baldwin, Florida, on May 17, 1865.
**First Commander:** Caraway Smith

*Field Officers:* Robert Harrison (Major)

Abner H. McCormick (Lieutenant Colonel)

*Assignments:* District of East Florida, Department of South Carolina, Georgia and Florida (Companies B, C, F, H and K) (December 1862-February 1864)

District of Middle Florida, Department of South Carolina, Georgia and Florida (Companies A, D, E, G and I) (December 1862-February 1864)

Cavalry, District of East Florida, Department of South Carolina, Georgia and Florida (February 1864)

District of Florida, Department of South Carolina, Georgia and Florida (February-July 1864)

Jackson's-Miller's Brigade (District of Florida), Department of South Carolina, Georgia and Florida (July 1864-May 1865)

*Battles:* Jacksonville (March 10, 1863)

near Jacksonville (March 23, 1863)

Ocklockonnee Bay (Companies G and I) (March 24, 1863)

Palatka (Company H) (March 27, 1863)

St. John's Mill (August 19, 1863)

St. Augustine (December 30, 1863)

Capture of the USS *Columbine* (detachment) (May 23, 1864)

Trout Creek (July 15, 1864)

Gainesville (August 15-19, 1864)

Magnolia (October 24, 1864)

Olustee (February 20, 1864)

Station Four (February 13, 1865)

*Further Reading:* Dickison, Mary Elizabeth, *Dickison and His Men, Reminiscences of the War in Florida.* Dickison, John J., *Volume XI-Florida, Confederate Military History.*

## 13. FLORIDA 3RD CAVALRY BATTALION

*Organization:* Organized from four independent companies on May 11, 1863. Consolidated with Murphy's Alabama Cavalry Battalion and three independent companies on September 24, 1863, and designated as the 15th Confederate Cavalry Regiment.

*First Commander:* Thomas J. Myers (Major)

*Assignment:* Eastern Division, Department of the Gulf

## 14. FLORIDA 5TH CAVALRY BATTALION

*Organization:* Organized with four companies on October 9, 1863. Company E assigned on October 21, 1863, from a part of Company D, 2nd Cavalry Regiment. Company F assigned on November 30, 1863, from a part of Company I, 2nd Florida Cavalry Regiment. Companies G and H assigned on April 17,

1864. Company I assigned later. Battalion surrendered at Tallahassee, Florida, by Major General Samuel Jones, commanding the District of Florida, on May 10, 1865.

**First Commander:** George W. Scott (Major, Lieutenant Colonel)
**Field Officer:** William H. Milton
**Assignments:** District of Middle Florida, Department of South Carolina, Georgia and Florida (October 1863-February 1864)
District of Florida, Department of South Carolina, Georgia and Florida (February-July 1864)
Jackson's-Miller's Brigade (District of Florida), Department of South Carolina, Georgia and Florida (July 1864-May 1865)
**Battles:** Trout Creek (July 15, 1864)
Gainesville (August 15-19, 1864)
Magnolia (October 24, 1864)
Station Four (February 13, 1865)

## 15.   FLORIDA MARIANNA DRAGOONS CAVALRY COMPANY

**Organization:** Organized at Marianna on March 14, 1862. Mustered in there for three years or the war ca. April 26, 1862. Assigned, as Company B, to the 15th Confederate Cavalry Regiment ca. September 24, 1863.
**First Commander:** Richard L. Smith (Captain)
**Assignments:** Department of Middle and Eastern Florida (March-October 1862)
District of East and Middle Florida, Department of South Carolina, Georgia and Florida (October-November 1862)
District of Middle Florida, Department of South Carolina, Georgia and Florida (November 1862-September 1863)
**Battle:** St. Andrew's Bay, Florida (April 7, 1862)

## 16.   FLORIDA MURPHY'S CAVALRY BATTALION

*See:*   ALABAMA AND FLORIDA CAVALRY BATTALION

## 17.   FLORIDA PICKETT'S CAVALRY COMPANY

**Organization:** Organized in late 1861. Mustered in for 12 months at Camp Winttner, near Jacksonville, on November 11, 1861. Mustered out on March 31, 1862.
**First Commander:** James A. Pickett (Captain)
**Assignment:** Department of Middle and Eastern Florida (November 1861-March 1862)

# INFANTRY

## 18. FLORIDA 1ST (MCDONELL'S) INFANTRY BATTALION

*Organization:* Organized into four companies from reenlisting members of the 1st Infantry Regiment ca. February 1862. Merged with Confederate Guards (La.) Response Battalion ca. May 1, 1862, as the Florida and Confederate Guards Response Battalion. The two battalions separated on July 17, 1862. This battalion merged into 1st Infantry Regiment (Reorganized) on August 15, 1862.

*First Commander:* Thaddeus A. McDonell (Major)

*Assignments:* Anderson's Brigade, Ruggles' Division, 2nd Corps, Army of the Mississippi, Department #2 (March-June 1862)

Anderson's Brigade, 2nd Corps, Army of the Mississippi, Department #2 (June-July 1862)

Anderson's Brigade, Jones' Division, Army of the Mississippi, Department #2 (July-August 1862)

*Battles:* Shiloh (April 6-7, 1862)

Farmington (May 1862)

Corinth Siege (May-June 1862)


## 19. FLORIDA 1ST SPECIAL INFANTRY BATTALION

*Organization:* Organized for 12 months as an artillery battalion of six companies on September 21, 1861. Converted to infantry on November 13, 1861. Reorganized on May 13, 1862. Consolidated with four companies of the 2nd Infantry Battalion on June 8, 1864, and designated at the 10th Infantry Regiment.

*First Commander:* Daniel P. Holland (Lieutenant Colonel)

*Field Officers:* Joseph Finegan (Lieutenant Colonel)

Charles F. Hopkins (Major, Lieutenant Colonel)

William W. Scott (Major)

*Assignments:* Department of Middle and East Florida (September 1861-November 1862)

District of Middle Florida, Department of South Carolina, Georgia and Florida
(November 1862-August 1863)
District of Georgia, Department of South Carolina, Georgia and Florida (August 1863-February 1864)
2nd Brigade, District of East Florida, Department of South Carolina, Georgia and Florida (February 1864)
District of Florida, Department of South Carolina, Georgia and Florida (February-May 1864)
Finegan's Brigade, Mahone's Division, 3rd Corps, Army of Northern Virginia (May-June 1864)
**Battles:**　St. John's Bluff, Florida (one company) (September 11, 1862)
near Jacksonville (March 25, 1863)
Olustee (February 20, 1864)
Cold Harbor (June 1-3, 1864)

## 20.　FLORIDA 1ST INFANTRY REGIMENT

**Organization:** Organized and mustered into Confederate service for 12 months at Chattahoochee on April 5, 1861. Failed at reorganization ca. February 1862. Men who reenlisted organized into four companies as the 1st (McDonell's) Infantry Battalion ca. February 1862.
**First Commander:**　J. Patton Anderson (Colonel)
**Field Officers:**　William H. Beard (Lieutenant Colonel)
Thaddeus A. McDonell (Major)
**Assignments:**　Department of West Florida (April-October 1861)
Department of Alabama and West Florida (October 1861)
Army of Pensacola, Department of Alabama and West Florida (October 1861-February 1862)
**Battle:**　Santa Rosa Island (October 9, 1861)

## 21.　FLORIDA 1ST (REORGANIZED) INFANTRY REGIMENT

**Organization:** Organized August 15, 1862, by the consolidation of the 1st (McDonell's) and 3rd (Miller's) Infantry Battalions. Field consolidation with the 3rd Infantry Regiment from December 1862 to April 9, 1865. Consolidated with 1st Cavalry Regiment and 3rd, 4th, 6th and 7th Infantry Regiments on April 9, 1865, at Smithfield, North Carolina, and designated as the 1st Infantry Regiment Consolidated.
**First Commander:**　William Miller (Colonel)
**Field Officers:**　Glover A. Ball (Major)
Henry Bradford (Major)
Thaddeus A. McDonell (Lieutenant Colonel)

*Assignments:*   Brown's Brigade, Anderson's Division, Left Wing, Army of the
   Mississippi, Department #2 (August-November 1862)
1st Brigade, Anderson Division, 2nd Corps, Army of Tennessee (November-
   December 1862)
Preston's Brigade, Breckinridge's Division, 2nd Corps, Army of Tennessee
   (December 1862-May 1863)
Preston's-Stovall's Brigade, Breckinridge's Division,  Department of the West
   (May-June 1863)
Stovall's Brigade, Breckinridge's Division, Department of Mississippi and East
   Louisiana (July-August 1863)
Stovall's-Florida Brigade, Breckinridge's-Bate's Division, 2nd Corps, Army of
   Tennessee (August 1863-February 1864)
Florida Brigade, Bate's Division, 1st Corps, Army of Tennessee (February
   1864-April 1865)
*Battles:*   Perryville (October 8, 1862)
Murfreesboro (December 31, 1862-January 3, 1863)
Jackson Siege (July 1863)
Chickamauga (September 19-20, 1863)
Chattanooga Siege (September-November 1863)
Atlanta Campaign (May-September 1864)
New Hope Church (May 25-June 5, 1864)
Atlanta (July 22, 1864)
Ezra Church (July 28, 1864)
Atlanta Siege (July-September 1864)
Jonesboro (August 31-September 1, 1864)
Franklin (November 30, 1864)
Nashville (December 15-16, 1864)
Carolinas Campaign (February-April 1865)

## 22.   FLORIDA 1ST INFANTRY REGIMENT RESERVES

*Organization:*   Organized from independent companies on January 5, 1865. Sur-
rendered by Major General Samuel Jones at Tallahassee, Florida, on May 10, 1865.
*First Commander:*   James J. Daniel (Colonel)
*Field Officers:*   William D. Barnes (Lieutenant Colonel)
William H. Dial (Major)
*Assignment:*   District of Florida, Department of South Carolina, Georgia and
Florida (January-May 1865)

## 23.   FLORIDA 1ST CONSOLIDATED INFANTRY REGIMENT

*Organization:*   Organized at Smithfield, North Carolina, on April 9, 1865, by
the consolidation of the 1st Cavalry Regiment, 1st Infantry Regiment (Reor-

ganized), and the 3rd, 4th, 6th and 7th Infantry Regiments. Surrendered at Durham Station, Orange County, North Carolina, on April 26, 1865.
**Field Officer:** Elisha Marshburn (Lieutenant Colonel)
**Assignment:** Smith's Brigade, Brown's Division, 1st Corps, Army of Tennessee (April 1865)
**Battle:** Carolinas Campaign (February-April 1865)

## 24. FLORIDA 2ND INFANTRY BATTALION

**Organization:** Original five companies mustered in for three years or the war between July 10, 1862, and August 14, 1862. Battalion itself organized on September 2, 1862, as the 1st Partisan Rangers Battalion. Company F mustered in and assigned to the battalion on February 17, 1863. Designation changed to 2nd Infantry Battalion on June 24, 1863. Battalion broken up on June 8, 1864. Four companies assigned to the new 10th Infantry Regiment and two companies to the new 11th Infantry Regiment.
**First Commander:** Theodore W. Brevard (Major, Lieutenant Colonel)
**Field Officer:** John Westcott (Major)
**Assignments:** Department of Middle and Eastern Florida (September-November 1862)
District of East Florida, Department of South Carolina, Georgia and Florida (November 1862-February 1864)
District of Florida, Department of South Carolina, Georgia and Florida (February-May 1864)
Finegan's Brigade, Mahone's Division, 3rd Corps, Army of Northern Virginia (May-June 1864)
**Battles:** St. John's Island, Florida (September 11, 1862)
Jacksonville (March 10, 1863)
St. Andrew's Bay, Florida (one company) (March 20, 1863)
near Jacksonville (March 25, 1863)
Fort Brooke (October 16, 1863)
Fort Brooke (December 25, 1863)
Cold Harbor (June 1-3, 1864)

## 25. FLORIDA 2ND INFANTRY REGIMENT

**Organization:** Organized by companies between April and July 1861. Mustered into Confederate service for 12 months near Jacksonville on July 13, 1861. Reorganized on May 11, 1862. Surrendered at Appomattox Court House, Virginia, on April 9, 1865.
**First Commander:** George T. Ward (Colonel)
**Field Officers:** William D. Ballantine (Major)
George W. Call (Major)

Walter R. Moore (Major, Lieutenant Colonel, Colonel)
Edward A. Perry (Colonel)
Lewis G. Pyles (Major, Lieutenant Colonel, Colonel)
Samuel St. George Rogers (Lieutenant Colonel)

**Assignments:** Unattached, Army of the Peninsula (September 1861)
Rains' Division, Army of the Peninsula (December 1861-April 1862)
Ward's Command, D. H. Hill's Division, Department of Northern Virginia (April-May 1862)
Garland's Brigade, D. H. Hill's Division, Department of Northern Virginia (May-June 1862)
Pryor's Brigade, Longstreet's Division, Army of Northern Virginia (June-July 1862)
Pryor's Brigade, Longstreet's Division, 1st Corps, Army of Northern Virginia (July-September 1862)
Pryor's-Perry's Brigade, Anderson's Division, 1st Corps, Army of Northern Virginia (September 1862-May 1863)
Perry's-Finegan's Brigade, Anderson's-Mahone's Division, 3rd Corps, Army of Northern Virginia (May 1863-April 1865)

**Battles:** Yorktown Siege (April-May 1862)
Williamsburg (May 5, 1862)
Seven Pines (May 31-June 1, 1862)
Seven Days Battles (June 25-July 1, 1862)
Beaver Dam Creek (June 26, 1862)
Gaines' Mill (June 27, 1862)
Frayser's Farm (June 30, 1862)
2nd Bull Run (August 28-30, 1862)
Antietam (September 17, 1862)
Fredericksburg (December 13, 1862)
Chancellorsville (May 1-4, 1863)
Gettysburg (July 1-3, 1863)
Bristoe Campaign (October 1863)
Mine Run Campaign (November-December 1863)
The Wilderness (May 5-6, 1864)
Spotsylvania Court House (May 8-21, 1864)
North Anna (May 22-26, 1864)
Cold Harbor (June 1-3, 1864)
Petersburg Siege (June 1864-April 1865)
Weldon Railroad (June 23, 1864)
Reams' Station (June 30, 1864)
Weldon Railroad (August 21, 1864)
Bellfield (December 9, 1864)
Hatcher's Run (February 5-7, 1865)

Farmville (April 7, 1865)
Appomattox Court House (April 9, 1865)
*Further Reading:*  Fleming, Francis Philip, *Memoir of Captain C. Seton Fleming of the 2nd Florida Infantry, C.S.A.*

## 26.  FLORIDA 3RD (MILLER'S) INFANTRY BATTALION

*Organization:*  This battalion of four companies organized in 1862 and also known as the 1st (Miller's) Infantry Battalion. Two companies presumably added later in the year. Consolidated with the 1st (McDonell's) Infantry Battalion on August 15, 1862.
*First Commander:*  William Miller (Lieutenant Colonel)

## 27.  FLORIDA 3RD INFANTRY REGIMENT

*Organization:*  Organized on July 25, 1861. Mustered into Confederate service for 12 months on Amelia Island on August 11, 1861. Reorganized on May 10, 1862. Served in a field consolidation with the 1st Infantry (Reorganized) Regiment from December 1862 to April 1865. Consolidated with the 1st Cavalry Regiment and the 1st (Reorganized), 4th, 6th and 7th Infantry Regiments and desginated as the 1st Consolidated Infantry Regiment on April 9, 1865 at Smithfield, North Carolina.
*First Commander:*  William S. Dilworth (Colonel)
*Field Officers:*  Lucius A. Church (Major, Lieutenant Colonel)
Elisha Marshburn (Major)
Jonathan L. Phillips (Major)
Arthur J. T. Wright (Lieutenant Colonel)
*Assignments:*  Department of Middle and Eastern Florida (August 1861-May 1862)
Brown's Brigade, Anderson's Division, Left Wing, Army of the Mississippi, Department #2 (August-November 1862)
1st Brigade, Anderson's Division, 2nd Corps, Army of Tennessee (November-December 1862)
Preston's Brigade, Breckinridge's Division, 2nd Corps, Army of Tennessee (December 1862-May 1863)
Preston's-Stovall's Brigade, Breckinridge's Division, Department of the West (May-July 1863)
Stovall's Brigade, Breckinridge's Division, Department of Mississippi and East Louisiana (July-August 1863)
Stovall's-Florida Brigade, Breckinridge's-Bate's Division, 2nd Corps, Army of Tennessee (August 1863-February 1864)
Florida Brigade, Bate's Division, 1st Corps, Army of Tennessee (February 1864-April 1865)
*Battles:*  Smyrna, Florida (March 23, 1862)

Brick Church, Florida (March 24, 1862)
Perryville (October 8, 1862)
Murfreesboro (December 31, 1862-January 3, 1863)
Jackson Siege (July 1863)
Chickamauga (September 19-20, 1863)
Chattanooga Siege (September-November 1863)
Chattanooga (November 23-25, 1863)
Atlanta Campaign (May-September 1864)
New Hope Church (May 25-June 5, 1864)
Atlanta (July 22, 1864)
Ezra Church (July 28, 1864)
Atlanta Siege (July-September 1864)
Jonesboro (August 31-September 1, 1864)
Franklin (November 30, 1864)
Nashville (December 15-16, 1864)
Carolinas Campaign (February-April 1865)
Bentonville (March 19-21, 1865)

## 28.  FLORIDA 4TH INFANTRY BATTALION

*Organization:*  Organized with seven companies on May 2, 1863. Consolidated with two companies of the 2nd Infantry Battalion and one independent company and designated as the 11th Infantry Regiment on June 8, 1864.
*First Commander:*  James F. McClellan (Lieutenant Colonel)
*Field Officer:*  John H. Gee (Major)
*Assignments:*  District of Middle Florida, Department of South Carolina, Georgia and Florida (June 1863-February 1864)
District of Florida, Department of South Carolina, Georgia and Florida (February-May 1864)
Finegan's Brigade, Mahone's Division, 3rd Corps, Army of Northern Virginia (May-June 1864)
*Battle:*  Cold Harbor (June 1-3, 1864)

## 29.  FLORIDA 4TH INFANTRY REGIMENT

*Organization:*  Organized in June 1861. Mustered into state service on July 1, 1861. Mustered into Confederate service by companies for 12 months between August 27 and October 24, 1861. The cavalry company originally attached to this regiment was later assigned to the 2nd Cavalry Regiment. Reorganized on May 12, 1862. Served in a field consolidation with the 1st Cavalry Regiment from November or December 1863 to April 1865. Consolidated with the 1st Cavalry Regiment and the 1st (Reorganized), 3rd, 6th and 7th Infantry Regi-

ments at Smithfield, North Carolina, on April 9, 1865, and designated as the
1st Infantry Regiment Consolidated.

**First Commander:**   Edward Hopkins (Colonel)

**Field Officers:**   Edward Badger (Major, Lieutenant Colonel)
Wiles L. L. Bowen (Major, Lieutenant Colonel, Colonel)
James P. Hunt (Colonel)
Jacob A. Lash (Major)
John T. Lesley (Major)
M. Whitt Smith (Lieutenant Colonel)

**Assignments:**   Department of Middle and Eastern Florida (August 1861-May
   1862)
Provost Guard, Army of Mobile, Department of Alabama and West Florida
   (May-June 1862)
District of the Gulf, Department #2 (July 1862)
Palmer's Brigade, Army of Middle Tennessee, Department #2 (October-No-
   vember 1862)
Palmer's Brigade, Breckinridge's Division, 1st Corps, Army of Tennessee (No-
   vember-December 1862)
Palmer's Brigade, Breckinridge's Division, 2nd Corps, Army of Tennessee
   (December 1862)
Preston's Brigade, Breckinridge's Division, 2nd Corps, Army of Tennessee
   (December 1862-May 1863)
Preston's-Stovall's Brigade, Breckinridge's Division, Department of the West
   (May-July 1863)
Stovall's Brigade, Breckinridge's Division, Department of Mississippi and East
   Louisiana (July-August 1863)
Stovall's-Florida Brigade, Breckinridge's-Bate's Division, 2nd Corps, Army of
   Tennessee (August 1863-February 1864)
Florida Brigade, Bate's Division, 1st Corps, Army of Tennessee (February
   1864-April 1865)

**Battles:**   Lebanon Pike, Tennessee (December 28, 1862)
Murfreesboro (December 31, 1862-January 3, 1863)
Jackson Siege (July 1863)
Chickamauga (September 19-20, 1863)
Chattanooga Siege (September-November 1863)
Chattanooga (November 23-25, 1863)
Atlanta Campaign (May-September 1864)
New Hope Church (May 25-June 5, 1864)
Atlanta (July 22, 1864)
Ezra Church (July 28, 1864)
Atlanta Siege (July-September 1864)

Jonesboro (August 31-September 1, 1864)
Franklin (November 30, 1864)
Nashville (December 15-16, 1864)
Carolinas Campaign (February-April 1865)
Bentonville (March 19-21, 1865)

## 30.  FLORIDA 5TH INFANTRY REGIMENT

**Organization:**  Mustered into Confederate service for three years on May 14, 1862. Organized for the war at Camp Leon on April 8, 1862. Surrendered at Appomattox Court House, Virginia, on April 9, 1865.

**First Commander:**  John C. Hateley (Colonel)

**Field Officers:**  Benjamin F. Davis (Major)
Thompson B. Lamar (Lieutenant Colonel, Major)

**Assignments:**  Department of Middle and Eastern Florida (April-July 1862)
Pryor's Brigade, Longstreet's Division, 1st Corps, Army of Northern Virginia (August-September 1862)
Pryor's-Perry's Brigade, Anderson's Division, 1st Corps, Army of Northern Virginia (September 1862-May 1863)
Perry's-Finegan's Brigade, Anderson's-Mahone's Division, 3rd Corps, Army of Northern Virginia (May 1863-April 1865)

**Battles:**  2nd Bull Run (August 28-30, 1862)
Antietam (September 17, 1862)
Fredericksburg (December 13, 1862)
Chancellorsville (May 1-4, 1863)
Gettysburg (July 1-3, 1863)
Bristoe Campaign (October 1863)
Mine Run Campaign (November-December 1863)
The Wilderness (May 5-6, 1864)
Spotsylvania Court House (May 8-21, 1864)
North Anna (May 22-26, 1864)
Cold Harbor (June 1-3, 1864)
Petersburg Siege (June 1864-April 1865)
Weldon Railroad (June 23, 1864)
Reams' Station (June 30, 1864)
Weldon Railroad (August 21, 1864)
Bellfield (December 9, 1864)
Hatcher's Run (February 5-7, 1865)
Farmville (April 7, 1865)
Appomattox Court House (April 9, 1865)

## 31.  FLORIDA 6TH INFANTRY BATTALION

*Organization:*  Organized from seven independent companies at Olustee on September 11, 1863. Increased to a regiment and designated as the 9th Infantry Regiment on April 28, 1864.

*First Commander:*  John M. Martin (Lieutenant Colonel)

*Field Officer:*  Pickens B. Bird (Major)

*Assignments:*  District of East Florida, Department of South Carolina, Georgia and Florida (September 1863-February 1864)

1st Brigade, District of East Florida, Department of South Carolina, Georgia and Florida (February 1864)

District of Florida, Department of South Carolina, Georgia and Florida (February-April 1864

*Battle:*  Olustee (February 20, 1864)


## 32.  FLORIDA 6TH INFANTRY REGIMENT

*Organization:*  Individual companies mustered into Confederate service for three years between March 14 and April 14, 1862. Regiment organized at Chattahoochee on April 14, 1862. Surrendered at Appomattox Court House, Virginia, on April 9, 1865.

*First Commander:*  Jesse J. Finley (Colonel)

*Field Officers:*  Robert H. M. Davidson (Major, Lieutenant Colonel)

Daniel L. Kenan (Major, Lieutenant Colonel, Colonel)

Angus D. McLean (Lieutenant Colonel, Colonel)

*Assignments:*  Department of Middle and Eastern Florida (April-June 1862)

Unattached, Department of East Tennessee (June-July 1862)

Davis' Brigade, Heth's Division, Department of East Tennessee (July-December 1862)

Davis'-Jackson's-Maxwell's-Trigg's Brigade, Department of East Tennessee (December 1862-September 1863)

Trigg's Brigade, Preston's Division, Buckner's Corps, Army of Tennessee (September-October 1863)

Trigg's Brigade, Buckner's Division, 1st Corps, Army of Tennessee (October-November 1863)

Florida Brigade, Bate's Division, 2nd Corps, Army of Tennessee (November 1863-February 1864)

Florida Brigade, Bate's Division, 1st Corps, Army of Tennessee (February 1864-April 1865)

*Battles:*  Chickamauga (September 19-20, 1863)

Chattanooga Siege (September-November 1863)

Chattanooga (November 23-25, 1863)

Atlanta Campaign (May-September 1864)

New Hope Church (May 25-June 5, 1864)
Dallas (May 28, 1864)
Atlanta (July 22, 1864)
Ezra Church (July 28, 1864)
Atlanta Siege (July-September 1864)
Jonesboro (August 31-September 1, 1864)
Franklin (November 30, 1864)
Nashville (December 15-16, 1864)
Carolinas Campaign (February-April 1865)
Bentonville (March 19-21, 1865)

## 33.  FLORIDA 7TH INFANTRY REGIMENT

*Organization:*  Organized at Gainesville on April 26, 1862. Mustered into Confederate service in April 1862. Consolidated with 1st Cavalry Regiment, 1st Infantry Regiment Reorganized and 3rd, 4th and 6th Infantry Regiments on April 9, 1865, at Smithfield, North Carolina, and designated as the 1st Infantry Regiment Consolidated.

*First Commander:*  Madison S. Perry (Colonel)

*Field Officers:*  Nathan S. Blount (Major)

Robert Bullock (Lieutenant Colonel, Colonel)

Tillman Ingram (Major, Lieutenant Colonel)

*Assignments:*  Post of Chattanooga, Department of East Tennessee (June-July 1862)

Davis' Brigade, Heth's Division, Department of East Tennessee (July-December 1862)

Davis'-Jackson's-Maxwell's-Trigg's Brigade, Department of East Tennessee (December 1862-September 1863)

Trigg's Brigade, Preston's Division, Buckner's Corps, Army of Tennessee (September-October 1863)

Trigg's Brigade, Buckner's Division, 1st Corps, Army of Tennessee (October-November 1863)

Florida Brigade, Bate's Division, 2nd Corps, Army of Tennessee (November 1863-February 1864)

Florida Brigade, Bate's Division, 1st Corps, Army of Tennessee (February 1864-April 1865)

*Battles:*  Chickamauga (September 19-20, 1863)

Chattanooga Siege (September-November 1863)

Chattanooga (November 23-25, 1863)

Atlanta Campaign (May-September 1864)

New Hope Church (May 25-June 5, 1864)

Ezra Church (July 28, 1864)

Atlanta Siege (July-September 1864)
Jonesboro (August 31-September 1, 1864)
Franklin (November 30, 1864)
Nashville (December 15-16, 1864)
Carolinas Campaign (February-April 1865)
Bentonville (March 19-21, 1865)

## 34.  FLORIDA 8TH INFANTRY REGIMENT

*Organization:*   Organized on July 5, 1862. Individual companies mustered into
Confederate service for three years between May 8 and July 4, 1862. Surren-
dered at Appomattox Court House, Virginia, on April 9, 1865.
*First Commander:*   Richard F. Floyd (Colonel)
*Field Officers:*   William Baya (Lieutenant Colonel)
Thomas E. Clarke (Major)
David Lang (Colonel)
John M. Pons (Lieutenant Colonel)
William J. Turner (Major)
*Assignments:*   Pryor's Brigade, Longstreet's Division, 1st Corps, Army of
    Northern Virginia (August-September 1862)
Pryor's-Perry's Brigade, Anderson's Division, 1st Corps, Army of Northern
    Virginia (September 1862-May 1863)
Perry's-Finegan's Brigade, Anderson's-Mahone's Division, 3rd Corps, Army of
    Northern Virginia (May 1863-April 1865)
*Battles:*   2nd Bull Run (August 28-30, 1862)
Antietam (September 17, 1862)
Fredericksburg (December 13, 1862)
Chancellorsville (May 1-4, 1863)
Gettysburg (July 1-3, 1863)
Bristoe Campaign (October 1863)
Bristoe Station (October 14, 1863)
Mine Run Campaign (November-December 1863)
The Wilderness (May 5-6, 1864)
Spotsylvania Court House (May 8-21, 1864)
North Anna (May 22-26, 1864)
Cold Harbor (June 1-3, 1864)
Petersburg Siege (June 1864-April 1865)
Weldon Railroad (June 23, 1864)
Reams' Station (June 30, 1864)
Weldon Railroad (August 21, 1864)
Bellfield (December 9, 1864)
Hatcher's Run (February 5-7, 1865)

Farmville (April 7, 1865)
Appomattox Court House (April 9, 1865)

## 35.   FLORIDA 9TH INFANTRY REGIMENT

**Organization:**  Organized by the consolidation of the 6th Infantry Battalion and three independent companies on April 28, 1864. Surrendered at Appomattox Court House, Virginia, on April 9, 1865.

**First Commander:**  John M. Martin (Colonel)

**Field Officers:**  Pickens B. Bird (Major)
Robert B. Thomas (Colonel) (acting)

**Assignment:**  Perry's-Finegan's Brigade, Anderson's-Mahone's Division, 3rd Corps, Army of Northern Virginia (May 1864-April 1865)

**Battles:**  Cold Harbor (June 1-3, 1864)
Petersburg Siege (June 1864-April 1865)
Weldon Railroad (June 23, 1864)
Reams' Station (June 30, 1864)
Weldon Railroad (August 21, 1864)
Bellfield (December 9, 1864)
Hatcher's Run (February 5-7, 1865)
Farmville (April 7, 1865)
Appomattox Court House (April 9, 1865)

## 36.   FLORIDA 10TH INFANTRY REGIMENT

**Organization:**  Organized by the consolidation of the 1st Special Infantry Battalion and four companies of the 2nd Infantry Battalion on June 8, 1864. Surrendered at Appomattox Court House, Virginia, on April 9, 1865.

**First Commander:**  Charles F. Hopkins (Colonel)

**Field Officers:**  William W. Scott (Lieutenant Colonel)
John Westcott (Major)

**Assignment:**  Perry's-Finegan's Brigade, Anderson's-Mahone's Division, 3rd Corps, Army of Northern Virginia (June 1864-April 1865)

**Battles:**  Petersburg Siege (June 1864-April 1865)
Weldon Railroad (June 23, 1864)
Reams' Station (June 30, 1864)
Weldon Railroad (August 21, 1864)
Bellfield (December 9, 1864)
Hatcher's Run (February 5-7, 1865)
Farmville (April 7, 1865)
Appomattox Court House (April 9, 1865)

### 37. FLORIDA 11TH INFANTRY REGIMENT

**Organization:** Organized by the consolidation of the 4th Infantry Battalion, two companies of the 2nd Infantry Battalion and one independent company on June 8, 1864. Surrendered at Appomattox Court House, Virginia, on April 9, 1865.

**First Commander:** Theodore W. Brevard (Colonel)

**Field Officers:** John H. Gee (Major)
James F. McClellan (Lieutenant Colonel)

**Assignment:** Perry's-Finegan's Brigade, Anderson's-Mahone's Division, 3rd Corps, Army of Northern Virginia (June 1864-April 1865)

**Battles:** Petersburg Siege (June 1864-April 1865)
Weldon Railroad (June 23, 1864)
Reams' Station (June 30, 1864)
Weldon Railroad (August 21, 1864)
Bellfield (December 9, 1864)
Hatcher's Run (February 5-7, 1865)
Farmville (April 7, 1865)
Appomattox Court House (April 9, 1865)

### 38. FLORIDA CAMPBELLTON BOYS INFANTRY COMPANY

**Organization:** Offered its services on July 15, 1861, but was rejected on July 29, 1861, due to a lack of arms.

**First Commander:** H. B. Grace (Captain)

The only Florida units engaged at Cold Harbor were the 2/5/8 consolidated regiment and the 6th Battalion. The 1st and 2nd battalions were not engaged, and the 4th battalion had not yet arrived

# ARKANSAS

# ARKANSAS UNITS

Arkansas seceded from the Union on May 6, 1861. Its troops were promptly transferred to the Confederate army.

One specialized type of unit was organized for the army: the State Troops, which were organized in June 1861 and were disbanded in September. Although several regiments did serve with the Confederate army at the Battle of Wilson's Creek on August 10, 1861, they never were transferred to Confederate service.

Because the state was largely overrun early in the war, no Local Defense Troops or Reserves units were organized.

One peculiarity of the state's numbering system was the repeated use of the same regimental numbers for several totally distinct units. Early in the war many of the state's regiments were transferred east of the Mississippi River. The state authorities then assigned the same numbers to new units raised for service west of the river. These units also frequently received a new regimental number whenever another colonel took command. I have tried to cite the number with which the regiment is most associated. The names of the various colonels follow the regimental number. Appropriate cross references are provided.

The state's artillery batteries received numerical designations on November 19, 1864.

Note: The index for the Arkansas units begins on page 131.

# ARTILLERY

## 1. ARKANSAS 1ST ARTILLERY BATTERY

*Organization:* Organized in September and October 1861. Apparently broken up in January 1864 with some of the men transferred to Cobb's Kentucky Battery.

*First Commander:* David Provence (Captain)

*Captains:* John T. Humphreys
John W. Rivers

*Assignments:* McCulloch's Division, Department #2 (October-December 1861)

Hébert's Brigade, McCulloch's Division, Department #2 (December1861-January 1862)

Hébert's Brigade, McCulloch's Division, Trans-Mississippi District, Department #2 (January-February 1862)

Artillery, McCulloch's Division, Trans-Mississippi District, Department #2 (February-March 1862)

Frost's Artillery Brigade, Price's Division, Trans-Mississippi District, Department #2 (March-April 1862)

Churchill's Brigade, McCown's Division, Army of the West, Department #2 (April-July 1862)

McNair's Brigade, McCown's Division, Department of East Tennessee (July-August 1862)

McNair's Brigade, McCown's Division, Army of Kentucky, Department #2 (August-October 1862)

McNair's Brigade, McCown's-Stewart's Division, E.K. Smith's Corps, Army of Tennessee (November 1862-March 1863)

McNair's Brigade, Stewart's Division, 1st Corps, Army of Tennessee (March-April 1863)

McNair's Brigade, Walker's Division, Department of the West (June 1863)

Clayton's Brigade, Stewart's Division, 2nd Corps, Army of Tennessee (July-August 1863)

Artillery Battalion, Stewart's Division, 2nd Corps, Army of Tennessee (August-September 1863)

Artillery Battalion, Stewart's Division, Buckner's Corps, Army of Tennessee (September 1863)

Artillery Battalion, Stewart's Division, 2nd Corps, Army of Tennessee (September-December 1863)

Atlanta, Georgia, Department of Tennessee (December 1863-January 1864)

**Battles:**  Pea Ridge (March 7, 1862)

Corinth Campaign (April-June 1862)

Farmington (May 9, 1862)

Richmond, Kentucky (August 29-30, 1862)

Murfreesboro (December 31, 1862-January 3, 1863)

Chickamauga (September 19-20, 1863)

Chattanooga Siege (September-November 1863)

Chattanooga (November 23-25, 1863)

## 2.  ARKANSAS 1ST FIELD ARTILLERY BATTERY

**Nickname:**  Arkansas Adams Artillery Battery

**Organization:**  Organized and mustered into state service in April 1861. Mustered into Confederate service on December 1, 1861. Reorganized ca. May 16, 1862. Regiment surrendered at Vicksburg, Warren County, Mississippi, on July 4, 1863. Paroled there later in month. Declared exchanged ca. November 1863. One section armed with two 3-inch Rifles between November 28, 1863, and January 5, 1864. Reorganized west of the Mississippi River ca. September 1864. Designated as the 1st Field Battery on November 19, 1864. Surrendered by General E. Kirby Smith, commanding the Trans-Mississippi Department, on May 26, 1865. Armed with four 6-lb. Smoothbores at the time of surrender.

**First Commander:**  James J. Gaines (Captain)

**Captain:**  Francis McNally

**Assignments:**  Hébert's Brigade, McCulloch's Division, Department #2 (December 1861-January 1862)

Hébert's Brigade, McCulloch's Division, Trans-Mississippi District, Department #2 (January-February 1862)

Artillery, McCulloch's Division, Trans-Mississippi District, Department #2 (February-March 1862)

Frost's Artillery Brigade, Price's Division, Trans-Mississippi District, Department #2 (March-April 1862)

Roane's-Phifer's Brigade, Jones'-Maury's Division, Army of the West, Department #2 (April-September 1862)

Phifer's Brigade, Maury's Division, Price's Corps, Army of West Tennessee, Department #2 (September-October 1862)

Phifer's Brigade, Maury's Division, Price's Corps, Army of West Tennessee, Department of Mississippi and East Louisiana (October-December 1862)

Light Artillery, 3rd Military District, Department of Mississippi and East Louisiana (January-February 1863)

Unattached, Maury's-Forney's Division, 2nd Military District, Department of Mississippi and East Louisiana (March-April 1863)

Unattached, Forney's Division, Department of Mississippi and East Louisiana (April 1863)

Shoup's Brigade, Smith's Division, Department of Mississippi and East Louisiana (April-July 1863)

Unattached, Department of Mississippi and East Louisiana (section) (November-December 1863)

Cosby's Brigade, Jackson's Division, Lee's Cavalry Corps, Department of Mississippi and East Louisiana (section) (December 1863)

Unattached, Department of Mississippi and East Louisiana (December 1863-January 1864)

5th (Blocher's) Light Artillery Battalion, 1st (Churchill's) Arkansas Division, 2nd Corps, Trans-Mississippi District (September 1864-May 1865)

**Battles:**   Pea Ridge (March 7-8, 1862)

Corinth (October 3-4, 1862)

Hatchie Bridge (October 7, 1862)

Oakland, Mississippi (December 3, 1862)

Vicksburg Campaign (May-July 1863)

Vicksburg Siege (May-July 1863)


## 3.   ARKANSAS 2ND FIELD ARTILLERY BATTERY

*Nickname:*   Arkansas Dallas (2nd Organization) Artillery Battery

*Organization:*   Organized as the successor the the Dallas Artillery (1st Organization) during June to August 1862. Armed with two 6-lb. Smoothbores and two 10-lb. Parrotts in January 1863. Surrendered at Arkansas Post on January 11, 1863. "Liberated" from Camp Butler, Illinois, prisoner-of-war camp in March 1863. Reorganized west of the Mississippi River in 1864. Designated as the 2nd Field Battery on November 19, 1864. Surrendered by General E. Kirby Smith, commanding the Trans-Mississippi Department, on May 26, 1865.

*First Commander:*   William Hart (Captain)

*Assignments:*   Garland's Brigade, 1st Corps, Army of the West, Trans-Mississippi Department (September-December 1862)

Garland's Brigade, Churchill's Division, 2nd Corps, Trans-Mississippi Department (December 1862)

Garland's Brigade, Churchill's Division, District of Arkansas, Trans-Mississippi Department (December 1862-January 1863)

Siege Train, Unattached, Trans-Mississippi Department (September-November 1864)

8th Light Artillery Battalion, Unattached, Trans-Mississippi Department (November 1864-May 1865)

**Battle:**  Arkansas Post (January 4-11, 1863)


## 4.  ARKANSAS 3RD FIELD ARTILLERY BATTERY

**Nicknames:**  Arkansas Pulaski Artillery Battery

Arkansas Little Rock Artillery Battery

**Organization:**  Organized and mustered into state service May 1861. Mustered into Confederate service July 15, 1861. Armed with two 6-lb. Smoothbores and two 12-lb. Smoothbores on August 10, 1861. Mustered out in late 1861. Reorganized and mustered into Confederate service on December 27, 1861. Designated as the 3rd Field Battery on November 19, 1864. Surrendered by General E. Kirby Smith, commanding the Trans- Mississippi Department, on May 26, 1865.

**First Commander:**  William E. Woodruff, Jr. (Captain)

**Captain:**  John G. Marshall

**Assignments:**  McCulloch's Brigade (August-September 1861)

McCulloch's Brigade, Department #2 (September 1861)

Department of the Indian Territory (May 1862)

District of the Indian Territory, Trans-Mississippi Department (May-August 1862)

District of Arkansas, Trans-Mississippi Department (August-December 1862)

McRae's Brigade, Shoup's Division, 1st Corps, Trans-Mississippi Department (December 1862-January 1863)

McRae's Brigade, Hindman's Division, District of Arkansas, Trans-Mississippi Department (January-February 1863)

Hill's Artillery Battalion, Unattached, District of Arkansas, Trans-Mississippi Department (April-May 1863)

McRae's-Churchill's Brigade, Price's Division, District of Arkansas, Trans-Mississippi Department (May 1863-March 1864)

Gause's Brigade, Arkansas Division, District of Arkansas, Trans-Mississippi Department (March-April 1864)

Gause's Brigade, Arkansas Division, Detachment from District of Arkansas, District of West Louisiana, Trans-Mississippi Department (April 1864)

Gause's Brigade, Arkansas Division, District of Arkansas, Trans-Mississippi Department (April-September 1864)

5th (Blocher's) Light Artillery Battalion, 1st (Churchill's) Arkansas Division, 2nd Corps, Trans-Mississippi Department (September 1864-January 1865)

Unattached Artillery, Trans-Mississippi Department (May 1865)

*Battles:* Wilson's Creek (August 10, 1861)
Helena (July 4, 1863)
Little Rock (September 10, 1863)
Red River Campaign (March-May 1864)
Camden Expedition (March-May 1864)

## 5. ARKANSAS 4TH FIELD ARTILLERY BATTERY

*Organization:* Organized in early 1862. Designated as the 4th Field Battery on November 19, 1864. Surrendered by General E. Kirby Smith, commanding the Trans-Mississippi Department, on May 26, 1865. Armed at the time of the surrender with one 3.67-inch Rifle, two 3-inch Rifles, and one 2.90-inch Rifle.
*First Commander:* Henry C. West (Captain)
*Assignments:* District of the Indian Territory, Department #2 (May 1862)
District of the Indian Territory, Trans-Mississippi Department (May 1862-March 1863)
Alexander's-Speight's Brigade, Steele's Division, District of Arkansas, Trans-Mississippi Department (March-May 1863)
District of West Louisiana, Trans-Mississippi Department (May 1863-September 1864)
5th (Blocher's) Light Artillery Battalion, 1st (Churchill's) Arkansas Division, 2nd Corps, Trans-Mississippi Department (September 1864-May 1865)
*Battles:* Red River Campaign (March-May 1864)

## 6. ARKANSAS 5TH FIELD ARTILLERY BATTERY

*Nicknames:* Arkansas Appeal Artillery Battery
Arkansas Memphis Appeal Artillery Battery
*Organization:* Organized at Memphis, Tennessee in April 1862. Regiment surrendered at Vicksburg, Warren County, Mississippi, on July 4, 1863. Paroled there later in month. Declared exchanged on December 20, 1863. Reorganized west of the Mississippi River in the summer of 1864. Designated as the 5th Field Battery on November 19, 1864. Surrendered by General E. Kirby Smith, commanding the Trans-Mississippi Department, on May 26, 1865. Armed at the time of the surrender with two 12-lb. Howitzers and two 6-lb. Smoothbores.
*First Commander:* W. C. Bryan (Captain)
*Captains:* William N. Hogg
Christopher C. Scott
*Assignments:* Rust's-Dockery's-Cabell's Brigade, Jones'-Maury's Division, Army of the West, Department #2 (April-September 1862)
Cabell's Brigade, Maury's Division, Price's Corps, Army of West Tennessee, Department #2 (September-October 1862)

Cabell's Brigade, Maury's Division, Price's Corps, Army of West Tennessee, Department of Mississippi and East Louisiana (October 1862)

Hébert's Brigade, Maury's Division, Price's Corps, Army of West Tennessee, Department of Mississippi and East Louisiana (Ocrober-December 1862)

Hébert's Brigade, Maury's Division, Price's Corps, Army of North Mississippi, Department of Mississippi and East Louisiana (December 1862-January 1863)

Hébert's Brigade, Maury's-Forney's Division, 2nd Military District, Department of Mississippi and East Louisiana (January-April 1863)

Hébert's Brigade, Forney's Division, Department of Mississippi and East Louisiana (April-July 1863)

8th Light Artillery Battalion, Unattached, Trans-Mississippi Department (September 1864-May 1865)

**Battles:** Corinth Campaign (April-June 1862)

Corinth (October 3-4, 1862)

Vicksburg Campaign (May-July 1863)

Vicksburg Siege (May-July 1863)

## 7. ARKANSAS 6TH FIELD ARTILLERY BATTERY

**Nickname:** Arkansas Washington Artillery Battery

**Organization:** Organized on June 14, 1862. Designated as the 6th Field Battery on November 19, 1864. Surrendered by General E. Kirby Smith, commanding the Trans-Mississippi Department, on May 26, 1865.

**First Commander:** Chambers B. Etter (Captain)

**Assignments:** Rains' Brigade, District of Arkansas, Trans-Mississippi Department (September-October 1862)

Bradfute's Brigade, Roane's Division 1st Corps, Trans-Mississippi Department (December 1862)

Shaver's-Tappan's Brigade, Hindman's-Price's Division, District of Arkansas, Trans-Mississippi Department (January-May 1863)

Artillery, Walker's Division, District of Arkansas, Trans-Mississippi Department (July-September 1863)

Fagan's-Tappan's Brigade, Price's Division, District of Arkansas, Trans-Mississippi Department (November 1863-March 1864)

Tappan's Brigade, Arkansas Division, District of Arkansas, Trans-Mississippi Department (March-April 1864)

Tappan's Brigade, Arkansas Division, Detachment from District of Arkansas, District of West Louisiana, Trans-Mississippi Department (April 1864)

Tappan's Brigade, Arkansas Division, District of Arkansas, Trans-Mississippi Department (April-September 1864)

8th Light Artillery Battalion, Unattached, Trans-Mississippi Department (September 1864-May 1865)

*Battles:*  Helena (July 4, 1863)
Little Rock (September 10, 1863)
Red River Campaign (March-May 1864)
Jenkins' Ferry (April 30, 1864)

## 8.  ARKANSAS 7TH FIELD ARTILLERY BATTERY

*Organization:*  Organized on August 6, 1862. Designated as the 7th Field Battery on November 19, 1864. Surrendered by General E. Kirby Smith, commanding the Trans-Mississippi Department, on May 26, 1865.
*First Commander:*  William D. Blocher (Captain)
*Captain:*  J. V. Zimmerman
*Assignments:*  Fagan's Brigade, Hindman's-Price's Division, District of Arkansas, Trans-Mississippi Department (January 1863)
Hill's Artillery Battalion, Price's Division, District of Arkansas, Trans-Mississippi Department (May 1863)
Fagan's Brigade, Price's Division, District of Arkansas, Trans-Mississippi Department (May 1863-January 1864)
Dobbin's Brigade, Fagan's Cavalry Division, District of Arkansas, Trans-Mississippi Department (April-August 1864)
Dobbin's Brigade, Fagan's Division, Price's Cavalry Corps (or Army of Missouri from September 18, 1864), Trans-Mississippi Department (section) (August-September 1864)
5th (Blocher's) Light Artillery Battalion, 1st (Churchill's) Arkansas Division, 2nd Corps, Trans-Mississippi Department (November 1864-May 1865)
*Battles:*  Helena (July 4, 1863)
Little Rock (September 10, 1863)
Camden Expedition (March-May 1864)
Price's Missouri Raid (September-October 1864)

## 9.  ARKANSAS 8TH FIELD ARTILLERY BATTERY

*Organization:*  Organized ca. April 1863. Not listed at the National Archives. Designated as the 8th Field Battery on November 19, 1864. Surrendered by General E. Kirby Smith, commanding the Trans-Mississippi Department, on May 26, 1865. Armed at the time of surrender with two 3-inch Rifles and two 12-lb. Howitzers.
*First Commander:*  William M. Hughey (Captain)
*Assignments:*  Cabell's Brigade, Steele's Division, District of Arkansas, Trans-Mississippi Department (April-December 1863)
Cabell's Brigade, Marmaduke's Cavalry Division, District of Arkansas, Trans-Mississippi Department (December 1863-January 1864)

Artillery, Fagan's Cavalry Division, District of Arkansas, Trans-Mississippi
Department (April-August 1864)
Cabell's Brigade, Fagan's Division, Price's Cavalry Corps (or Army of Missouri
from September 18, 1864), Trans-Mississippi Department (August-September 1864)
2nd (Pratt's) Horse Artillery Battalion, Price's Cavalry Corps (or Army of
Missouri from September 18, 1864), Trans-Mississippi Department (September 1864-May 1865)
**Battles:** Fayetteville (April 18, 1863)
Devil's Backbone (September 1, 1863)
Camden Expedition (March-May 1864)
Poison Springs (April 18, 1864)
Lake Chicot, Arkansas (June 6, 1864)
Price's Missouri Raid (September-October 1864)

## 10.  ARKANSAS ADAMS ARTILLERY BATTERY
*See:*  ARKANSAS 1ST FIELD ARTILLERY BATTERY

## 11.  ARKANSAS APPEAL ARTILLERY BATTERY
*See:*  ARKANSAS 5TH FIELD ARTILLERY BATTERY

## 12.  ARKANSAS CLARKE COUNTY ARTILLERY BATTERY
**Organization:**  Organized in Clarke County on July 15, 1861. Armed with two
6-lb. Smoothbores and two 12-lb. Howitzers between April 6, 1862, and
November 11, 1862. Reorganized on May 25, 1862. Served for a time as
Company E, 14th Georgia Artillery Battalion. Surrendered by General Joseph
E. Johnston at Durham Station, Orange County, North Carolina, on April 26,
1865.
**First Commander:**  Franklin Roberts (Captain)
**Captain:**  Jannedine H. Wiggins
**Assignments:**  Upper District of Arkansas (August-September 1861)
Upper District of Arkansas, Department #2 (September-December 1861)
Unattached Artillery, Army of the Mississippi, Department #2 (March-April
1862)
Shaver's-Liddell's Brigade, 3rd Corps, Army of the Mississippi, Department #2
(April-July 1862)
Liddell's Brigade, Buckner's Division, Army of the Mississippi, Department #2
(July-August 1862)
Liddell's Brigade, Buckner's Division, Left Wing, Army of the Mississippi,
Department #2 (August-October 1862)

Forrest's Cavalry Brigade, Army of Middle Tennessee, Department #2 (October-November 1862)

Forrest's Cavalry Brigade, Army of Tennessee (November-December 1862)

Wheeler's Brigade, Wheeler's Cavalry Division, Army of Tennessee (December 1862-March 1863)

Artillery, Martin's Division, Wheeler's Cavalry Corps, Army of Tennessee (March-November 1863)

Artillery, Martin's-Morgan's Division, Martin's Cavalry Corps, Department of East Tennessee (November 1863-February 1864)

Robertson's-Hamilton's Artillery Battalion, Wheeler's Cavalry Corps, Army of Tennessee (March-October 1864)

Artillery, Wheeler's Cavalry Corps, Department of South Carolina, Georgia and Florida (October 1864-February 1865)

Artillery, Wheeler's Cavalry Corps, Hampton's Cavalry Command (February-April 1865)

Artillery, Wheeler's Cavalry Corps, Hampton's Cavalry Command, Army of Tennessee (April 1865)

*Battles:* Shiloh (April 6-7, 1862)

Corinth (October 3-4, 1862)

Murfreesboro (December 31, 1862-January 3, 1863)

Tullahoma Campaign (June 1863)

Chickamauga (September 19-20, 1863)

Chattanooga Siege (September-November 1863)

Knoxville Siege (November 1863)

Atlanta Campaign (May-September 1864)

Atlanta Siege (July-September 1864)

Savannah Campaign (November-December 1864)

Carolinas Campaign (February-April 1865)

## 13.  ARKANSAS DALLAS (1ST ORGANIZATION) ARTILLERY BATTERY

*Organization:*  Organized on August 1, 1861. Disbanded "for shameful misconduct before the enemy at Elk Horn (Pea Ridge) March 8, 1862" on May 25, 1862.

*First Commander:*  William Hart (Captain)

*Assignments:*  McCulloch's Division, Department #2 (October-December 1861)

Hébert's Brigade, McCulloch's Division, Department #2 (December 1861-January 1862)

Hébert's Brigade, McCulloch's Division, Trans-Mississippi District, Department #2 (January-February 1862)

Artillery, McCulloch's Division, Trans-Mississippi District, Department #2 (February-March 1862)

Frost's Artillery Brigade, Price's Division, Trans-Mississippi District, Department #2 (March-April 1862)

**Battle:**  Pea Ridge (March 7-8, 1862)

## 14.  ARKANSAS DALLAS (2ND ORGANIZATION) ARTILLERY BATTERY

*See:*  ARKANSAS 2ND FIELD ARTILLERY BATTERY

## 15.  ARKANSAS DREW LIGHT ARTILLERY BATTERY

*See:*  ARKANSAS MONTICELLO ARTILLERY BATTERY

## 16.  ARKANSAS FORT SMITH ARTILLERY BATTERY

**Organization:**  Organized in state service at Fort Smith in 1861. Armed with four guns on August 10, 1861. Mustered out of state service in the late summer of 1861.

**First Commander:**  J. G. Reid (Captain)

**Assignment:**  Pearce's Arkansas State Troops Brigade (July-August 1861)

**Battle:**  Wilson's Creek (August 10, 1861)

## 17.  ARKANSAS HELENA ARTILLERY BATTERY

**Organization:**  Organized in state service on April 29, 1861. Mustered out of state service on July 4, 1861. Reorganized for Confederate service on July 6, 1861. Armed with two 12-lb. Howitzers and two 6-lb. Smoothbores on April 6-7, 1862. Armed with four 12-lb. Howitzers between March 29 and April 1, 1864. Battery served at times as Company C, 20th Alabama Light Artillery Battalion, and as Company H, 28th Georgia Artillery Battalion. Surrendered at Macon, Georgia, on April 21, 1865.

**First Commander:**  A. W. Clarkson (Captain)

**Captains:**  John H. Calvert

Thomas J. Key

**Assignments:**  Upper District of Arkansas (August-October 1861)

Artillery, Hardee's Division, Central Army of Kentucky, Department #2 (October 1861-March 1862)

Cleburne's Brigade, 3rd Corps, Army of the Mississippi, Department #2 (March-July 1862)

Cleburne's Brigade, Buckner's Division, Army of the Mississippi, Department #2 (July-August 1862)

Cleburne's Brigade, Buckner's Division, Left Wing, Army of the Mississippi, Department #2 (August 1862)

Cleburne's Brigade, Cleburne's Division, Army of Kentucky, Department #2 (August-October 1862)

Cleburne's Brigade, Buckner's Division, Left Wing, Army of the Mississippi, Department #2 (October-November 1862)

Cleburne's-Polk's Brigade, Buckner's-Cleburne's Division, 2nd Corps, Army of Tennessee (November 1862-August 1863)

Artillery Battalion, Cleburne's Division, 2nd Corps, Army of Tennessee (August-November 1863)

Artillery Battalion, Cleburne's Division, 1st Corps, Army of Tennessee (November 1863-February 1864)

Hotchkiss' Battalion, Artillery, 1st Corps, Army of Tennessee (February-December 1864)

District of Georgia, Department of Tennessee and Georgia (April 1865)

**Battles:**  Shiloh (April 6-7, 1862)

Corinth Campaign (April-June 1862)

Perryville (October 8, 1862)

Murfreesboro (December 31, 1862-January 3, 1863)

Tullahoma Campaign (June 1863)

Chickamauga (September 19-20, 1863)

Chattanooga Siege (September-November 1863)

Chattanooga (November 23-25, 1863)

Atlanta Campaign (May-September 1864)

Pickett's Mill (May 27, 1864)

Atlanta Siege (July-September 1864)

Nashville (December 15-16, 1864)

**Further Reading:**  Cate, Wirt Armistead, ed., *Two Soldiers, the Campaign Diaries of Thomas J. Key, C.S.A., December 7, 1863-May 17, 1865; and Robert J. Campbell, U.S.A., January 1, 1864-July 21, 1864.*

## 18.   ARKANSAS HOADLEY'S-PARKS' HEAVY ARTILLERY COMPANY

**Organization:**  Organized at Little Rock in October 1861. Became Company H, 1st Tennessee Heavy Artillery Regiment, on May 10, 1862.

**First Commander:**  Frederick W. Hoadley (Captain)

**Assignments:**  Stewart's Brigade, McCown's Division, 1st Geographical Division, Department #2 (February-March 1862)

Artillery, McCown's Command, 1st Geographical Division, Department #2 (March-May 1862)

**Battle:**  Island #10 (April 6-7, 1862)

## 19.   ARKANSAS JACKSON LIGHT ARTILLERY BATTERY

**Also Known As:**  Arkansas McCown Artillery Battery

**Organization:**  Organized in 1861. Mustered into state service at Jacksonport on June 15, 1861. Mustered into Confederate service on July 25, 1861. Armed with two 6-lb. Smoothbores and two 3-inch Rifles on April 67, 1862. Possibly consolidated with the Helena Artillery during the spring of 1862. Converted to heavy artillery service in 1862. Armed with four 6-lb. Smoothbores and two 3-inch Rifles on November 28, 1863. Armed with four 6-lb. Smoothbores and two 6-lb. Rifles on January 5, 1864. Armed with four 6-lb. Smoothbores in May 1864. Surrendered by General E. Kirby Smith, commanding the Trans-Mississippi Department, on May 26, 1865.

**First Commander:**  George W. McCown (Captain)

**Captains:**  George T. Hubbard
James G. Thrall

**Assignments:**  Upper District of Arkansas, Department #2 (August-September 1861)
Artillery, Hardee's Division, Central Army of Kentucky, Department #2 (October 1861-March 1862)
Cleburne's Brigade, 3rd Corps, Army of the Mississippi, Department #2 (March-May 1862)
1st Military District, Department of Mississippi and East Louisiana (October 1862-September 1863)
Ruggles' Command, Department of Mississippi and East Louisiana (September 1863-January 1864)
Ruggles' Command, Department of Alabama, Mississippi and East Louisiana (January-February 1864)
Artillery, Chalmers' Division, Forrest's Cavalry Corps, Department of Alabama, Mississippi and East Louisiana (February-May 1864)
Artillery, Forrest's Cavalry Corps, Department of Alabama, Mississippi and East Louisiana (May-November 1864)
Artillery, District of Mississippi and East Louisiana, Department of Alabama, Mississippi and East Louisiana (November-December 1864)
Hoxton's Artillery Battalion, Left Wing, Defenses of Mobile, Artillery Reserves, etc., Department of Alabama, Mississippi and East Louisiana (March-April 1865)
Hoxton's Artillery Battalion, Fuller's Regiment, Department of Alabama, Mississippi and East Louisiana (April-May 1865)

**Battles:**  Shiloh (April 6-7, 1862)
Corinth Campaign (April-June 1862)
Meridian Campaign (February-March 1864)
Yazoo City (March 5, 1864)
Tupelo (July 14, 1864)
A.J. Smith's 2nd Mississippi Invasion (August 1864)

Forrest's West Tennessee Raid (October 16-November 10, 1864)
Mobile (March 17-April 12, 1865)

## 20. ARKANSAS LITTLE ROCK ARTILLERY BATTERY

*See:* ARKANSAS 3RD FIELD ARTILLERY BATTERY

## 21. ARKANSAS MCCOWN ARTILLERY BATTERY

*See:* ARKANSAS JACKSON LIGHT ARTILLERY BATTERY

## 22. ARKANSAS MCCOWN GUARDS HEAVY ARTILLERY COMPANY

*Organization:* Organized possibly at Lamartine ca. December 6, 1861. Became 1st Company B, 1st Heavy Artillery, on May 10, 1862.

*First Commander:* Paul T. Dismukes (Captain)

*Assignments:* Stewart's Brigade, 1st Geographical Division, Department #2 (February 1862)

Gantt's Brigade, McCown's Command, 1st Geographical Division, Department #2 (February-March 1862)

Artillery, McCown's Command, 1st Geographical Division, Department #2 (March-May 1862)

*Battle:* Island #10 (April 6-7, 1862)

## 23. ARKANSAS MEMPHIS APPEAL ARTILLERY BATTERY

*See:* ARKANSAS 5TH FIELD BATTERY

## 24. ARKANSAS MONTICELLO ARTILLERY BATTERY

*Nickname:* Arkansas Drew Light Artillery Battery

*Organization:* Organized for one year on February 8, 1862. Reorganized for the war on May 15, 1862. Armed with five 6-lb. Smoothbores and one 3.3-inch Rifle between January 1, 1863, and November 28, 1863. Armed with two 6-lb. Smoothbores, one 3.3-inch Rifle and one 12-lb. Howitzer on May 1, 1864. Surrendered by General E. Kirby Smith, commanding the Trans-Mississippi Department, on May 26, 1865.

*First Commander:* James A. Owens (Captain)

*Captain:* W. C. Howell

*Assignments:* 1st Military District, Department of Mississippi and East Louisiana (October 1862-September 1863)

Ferguson's Brigade, Lee's Cavalry Corps, Department of Mississippi and East Louisiana (September 1863-January 1864)

Ferguson's Brigade, Jackson's Division, Lee's Cavalry Corps, Department of Mississippi and East Louisiana (January 1864)

Ferguson's Brigade, Jackson's Division, Lee's Cavalry Corps, Department of
     Alabama, Mississippi and East Louisiana (Janaury-May 1864)
Artillery, W. Adams' Cavalry Division, Department of Alabama, Mississippi
     and East Louisiana (May-June 1864)
Liddell's Brigade, District of the Gulf, Department of Alabama, Mississippi and
     East Louisiana (September-October 1864)
Artillery, Liddell's Division, District of the Gulf, Department of Alabama,
     Mississippi and East Louisiana (October-December 1864)
**Battle:**  Meridian Campaign (February-March 1864)

### 25.  ARKANSAS PINE BLUFF ARTILLERY BATTERY

**Organization:**  Organized between April and June 1861. Apparently became
Company S, 1st Infantry Battalion, during the summer of 1861.
**First Commander:**  Frederick P. Steck (Captain)
**Assignment:**  District of Arkansas (June-July 1861)

### 26.  ARKANSAS PULASKI ARTILLERY BATTERY

**See:**  ARKANSAS 3RD FIELD ARTILLERY BATTERY

### 27.  ARKANSAS WASHINGTON ARTILLERY BATTERY

**See:**  ARKANSAS 6TH FIELD BATTERY

# CAVALRY

## 28. ARKANSAS 1ST (PHIFER'S) CAVALRY BATTALION

*See:* ARKANSAS 6TH (PHIFER'S) CAVALRY BATTALION

## 29. ARKANSAS (AND LOUISIANA) 1ST CAVALRY BATTALION

*Organization:* Not listed in the *Official Records* or at the National Archives. Number of companies is undetermined.
*First Commander:* B. W. Buckner (Major) (acting)

## 30. ARKANSAS 1ST CAVALRY BATTALION RESERVES

*Organization:* Organized with an undetermined number of companies in late 1864. Not listed in the *Official Records* or at the National Archives.
*First Commander:* Flippin (Lieutenant Colonel)
*Field Officer:* S. T. Abbott (Major)

## 31. ARKANSAS 1ST (BORLAND'S) CAVALRY BATTALION

*Organization:* Organized with an undetermined number of companies in early 1861. Increased to a regiment and designated as the 1st Mounted Volunteers Regiment, later the 3rd Cavalry Regiment, on July 24, 1861.
*First Commander:* Solon Borland (Lieutenant Colonel)
*Assignment:* District of Arkansas (July 1861)

## 32. ARKANSAS 1ST (BROOKS'-STIRMAN'S) CAVALRY BATTALION

*Organization:* Organized with five companies in 1861. Dismounted ca. April 1862. Companies D, C and B, Williamson's Infantry Battalion, became Companies F, G and H, respectively, on May 25, 1862. Consolidated with Bridges' Sharpshooters Battalion and designated as Stirman's Sharpshooters Regiment on August 1, 1862. Soon reverted to its former designation. Battalion surrendered at Vicksburg, Warren County, Mississippi, on July 4, 1863. Paroled there later in month. Reorganized west of the Mississippi River in 1864. Surrendered by General E. Kirby Smith, commanding the Trans-Mississippi Department, on May 26, 1865.

**First Commander:** William H. Brooks (Major)

**Field Officer:** Ras. Stirman (Lieutenant Colonel)

**Assignments:** Hébert's Brigade, McCulloch's Division, Department #2 (December 1861-February 1862)

Unattached, Trans-Mississippi District, Department #2 (March 1862)

Steen's Brigade, Price's Division, Trans-Mississippi District, Department #2 (March-April 1862)

Phifer's Brigade, Maury's Division, Price's Corps, Army of West Tennessee, Department #2 (April-September 1862)

Phifer's Brigade, Maury's Division, Price's Corps, Army of West Tennessee, Department of Mississippi and East Louisiana (September-October 1862)

Hébert's Brigade, Bowen's Division, Price's Corps, Army of West Tennessee, Department of Mississippi and East Louisiana (October 1862)

Cravens' Brigade, Bowen's Division, Price's Corps, Army of West Tennessee, Department of Mississippi and East Louisiana (December 1862-January 1863)

Cravens'-Green's Brigade, Bowen's Division, 2nd Corps, Army of North Mississippi, Department of Mississippi and East Louisiana (December 1862-January 1863)

Green's Brigade, Bowen's Division, 2nd Corps, Army of North Mississippi, Department of Mississippi and East Louisiana (January-February 1863)

Green's Brigade, Forney's-Bowen's Division, 2nd Military District, Department of Mississippi and East Louisiana (March-April 1863)

Green's Brigade, Bowen's Division, Department of Mississippi and East Louisiana (April-July 1863)

2nd (Slemons'-Crawford's) Cavalry Brigade, Arkansas (Fagan's) Cavalry Division, Price's Cavalry Corps, Trans-Mississippi Department (September 1864-May 1865)

**Battles:** Pea Ridge (March 7-8, 1862)

Corinth Campaign (April-June 1862)

Corinth (October 3-4, 1862)

Grand Gulf (April 29, 1863)

Port Gibson (May 1, 1863)

Vicksburg Campaign (May-July 1863)

Champion Hill (May 16, 1863)

Big Black River Bridge (May 17, 1863)

Vicksburg Siege (May-July 1863)

Scout from Waldron to Mount Ida, Caddo Gap and Dallas (December 2-7, 1863)

Price's Missouri Raid (September-October 1864)
Ivey's Ford (January 17, 1865)
**Further Reading:** McCollom, Albert O., *The War-time Letters of Albert O. McCollom.*

### 33. ARKANSAS 1ST CAVALRY REGIMENT MOUNTED RIFLES

**Organization:** Mustered by companies into Confederate service on June 9-15, 1861. Organized on June 16, 1861. Dismounted in April 1862. Reorganized on May 1, 1862. Consolidated with the 2nd Mounted Rifles Regiment, 4th Infantry Battalion and 4th, 9th and 25th Infantry Regiments and designated as the 1st Mounted Rifles Regiment Consolidated at Smithfield, North Carolina, on April 9, 1865.

**First Commander:** Thomas J. Churchill (Colonel)

**Field Officers:** William P. Campbell (Major)

Morton G. Galloway (Lieutenant Colonel)

Robert W. Harper (Major, Colonel)

George S. Laswell (Major, Lieutenant Colonel)

Charles H. Matlock (Lieutenant Colonel)

Leander M. Ramsaur (Major, Lieutenant Colonel, Colonel)

Daniel H. Reynolds (Major, Lieutenant Colonel, Colonel)

George W. Wells (Major, Lieutenant Colonel)

**Assignments:** McCulloch's Brigade (August 1861)

Indian Territory (September-October 1861)

McCulloch's Division, Department #2 (October-December 1861)

McIntosh's Brigade, McCulloch's Division, Department #2 (December 1861-January 1862)

McIntosh's Brigade, McCulloch's Division, Trans-Mississippi District, Department #2 (January-March 1862)

Churchill's Cavalry Brigade, Price's Division, Trans-Mississippi District, Department #2 (March-April 1862)

Churchill's Brigade, McCown's Division, Army of the West, Department #2 (April-July 1862)

McNair's Brigade, McCown's Division, Department of East Tennessee (July-December 1862)

NcNair's Brigade, McCown's Division, E. K. Smith's Corps, Army of Tennessee (December 1862-March 1863)

McNair's Brigade, McCown's Division, 1st Corps, Army of Tennessee (March-April 1863)

McNair's Brigade, Walker's Division, Department of the West (June 1863)

McNair's Brigade, French's Division, Department of the West (June-July 1863)

McNair's Brigade, French's Division, Department of Mississippi and East Louisiana (July-September 1863)

McNair's Brigade, Johnson's Provisional Division, Army of Tennessee (September 1863)

McNair's Brigade, French's Division, Department of Mississippi and East Louisiana (Setpember 1863-January 1864)

McNair's Brigade, French's Division, Department of Alabama, Mississippi and East Louisiana (January-February 1864)

McNair's-D. H. Reynolds' Brigade, Department of the Gulf (February-April 1864)

D. H. Reynolds' Brigade, District of the Gulf, Department of Alabama, Mississippi and East Louisiana (April-May 1864)

D. H. Reynolds' Brigade, Cantey's-Walthall's Division, Army of Mississippi (May-July 1864)

D. H. Reynolds' Brigade, Walthall's Division, 3rd Corps, Army of Tennessee (July 1864-April 1865)

**Battles:**  Nesho, Missouri (July 5, 1861)
Wilson's Creek (August 10, 1861)
Pea Ridge (March 7-8, 1862)
Richmond, Kentucky (August 29-30, 1862)
Murfreesboro (December 31, 1862-January 3, 1863)
Jackson Siege (July 1863)
Chickamauga (September 19-20, 1863)
Chattanooga Siege (September-November 1863)
Atlanta Campaign (May-September 1864)
Dug Gap (May 8, 1864)
Resaca (May 14-15, 1864)
Peach Tree Creek (July 20, 1864)
Atlanta (July 22, 1864)
Ezra Church (July 28, 1864)
Atlanta Siege (July-September 1864)
Jonesboro (August 31-September 1, 1864)
Lovejoy's Station (September 2-5, 1864)
Moon's Station (October 4, 1864)
Franklin (November 30, 1864)
Nashville (December 15-16, 1864)
Sugar Creek (December 26, 1864)
Carolinas Campaign (February-April 1865)
Bentonville (March 19-21, 1865)

**Further Reading:**  Dacus, Robert H., *Reminiscences of Company "H," First Arkansas Mounted Rifles.*

## 34. ARKANSAS 1ST CAVALRY REGIMENT MOUNTED RIFLES CONSOLIDATED

*Organization:* Organized by the consolidation of the 1st and 2nd Mounted Rifles Regiments, the 4th Infantry Battalion and the 4th, 9th and 25th Infantry Regiments at Smithfield, North Carolina, on April 9, 1865. Surrendered by General Joseph E. Johnston at Durham Station, Orange County, North Carolina, on April 26, 1865.

*First Commander:* Henry G. Bunn (Colonel)

*Assignment:* Featherston's Brigade, Loring's Division, 3rd Corps, Army of Tennessee (April 1865)

*Battle:* Carolinas Campaign (February-April 1865)

## 35. ARKANSAS 1ST CAVALRY REGIMENT MOUNTED VOLUNTEERS

*See:* ARKANSAS 3RD CAVALRY REGIMENT

## 36. ARKANSAS 1ST CAVALRY REGIMENT STATE TROOPS

*Organization:* Organized in 1861. Mustered out on September 19, 1861. Subsequently reorganized as the 1st (Carroll's-Thompson's) Cavalry Regiment.

*First Commander:* De Rosey Carroll (Colonel)

*Assignment:* Pearce's Arkansas State Troops Brigade (August-September 1861)

*Battle:* Wilson's Creek (August 10, 1861)

## 37. ARKANSAS 1ST (CARROLL'S-THOMSON'S) CAVALRY REGIMENT

*Organization:* Organized as the successor to the 1st Cavalry Regiment, State Troops, in 1862. Company served detached as escort to Colonel, later Brigadier General, Charles A. Carroll from March 10, 1863. Became the 4th (Gordon's) Cavalry Regiment on December 15, 1863.

*First Commander:* Charles A. Carroll (Colonel)

*Field Officers:* J. A. Johnson (Lieutenant Colonel)

Lee L. Thomson (Lieutenant Colonel, Colonel)

*Assignments:* Cabell's Cavalry Brigade, District of Arkansas, Trans-Mississippi Department (April 1863)

Cabell's Cavalry Brigade, District of the Indian Territory, Trans-Mississippi Department (April 1863)

*Battles:* Cane Hill (November 28, 1862)

Prairie Grove (December 7, 1862)

Marmaduke's Expedition into Missouri (December 31, 1862-January 25, 1863)

Fayetteville (April 18, 1863)

Devil's Backbone (September 1, 1863)

## 38. ARKANSAS 1ST (CRAWFORD'S) CAVALRY REGIMENT

*Also Known As:* 10th (Crawford's) Cavalry Regiment
*Organization:* Organized with 12 companies at Camden on December 30, 1863. Surrendered by General E. Kirby Smith, commanding the Trans-Mississippi Department, on May 26, 1865.
*First Commander:* William A. Crawford (Colonel)
*Field Officers:* Dawson L. Kilgore (Lieutenant Colonel)
John W. Walker (Major)
*Assignments:* Crawford's-Slemons' Brigade, Fagan's Cavalry Division, District of Arkansas, Trans-Mississippi Department (April-September 1864)
2nd (Slemons'-Crawford's) Arkansas Cavalry Brigade, 1st (Fagan's) Arkansas Cavalry Division, Price's Cavalry Corps (or Army of Missouri), Trans-Mississippi Department (September 1864-May 1865)
*Battles:* Camden Expedition (March-May 1864)
Poison Springs (April 18, 1864)
Marks' Mill (April 25, 1864)
Price's Missouri Raid (September-October 1864)

## 39. ARKANSAS 1ST (DOBBIN'S) CAVALRY REGIMENT

*Organization:* Organized by the increasing of Chrisman's Cavalry Battalion to a regiment in early 1863. No record of Companies I and K ever being formed. Apparently broken up and the men assigned to the 2nd (Morgan's) Cavalry Regiment on January 3, 1864.
*First Commander:* Archibald S. Dobbin (Colonel)
*Field Officer:* Samuel M. Corley (Major)
*Assignments:* Unattached, District of Arkansas, Trans-Mississippi Department (May 1863)
Arkansas Cavalry Brigade, Walker's Division, District of Arkansas, Trans-Mississippi Department (June-September 1863)
Dobbin's Cavalry Brigade, District of Arkansas, Trans-Mississippi Department (November 1863)
*Battles:* Helena (July 4, 1863)
Little Rock (September 10, 1863)
Pine Bluff (October 25, 1863)

## 40. ARKANSAS 1ST (FAGAN'S-MONROE'S) CAVALRY REGIMENT

*Also Known As:* Arkansas 6th (Fagan's-Monroe's) Cavalry Regiment
*Organization:* Organized by the increasing of Johnson's Cavalry Battalion to a regiment in 1862. 13th Cavalry Battalion temporarily attached to this regiment in 1864. Surrendered by General E. Kirby Smith, commanding the Trans-Mississippi Department, on May 26, 1865.

*First Commander:* James F. Fagan (Colonel)
*Field Officers:* M. D. Davis (Major)
James C. Monroe (Lieutenant Colonel, Colonel)
James M. O'Neil (Major, Lieutenant Colonel)
A. V. Reiff (Major, Lieutenant Colonel)
*Assignments:* District of Arkansas, Trans-Mississippi Department (November-December 1862)
Carroll's Brigade, Marmaduke's Cavalry Division, 1st Corps, Trans-Mississippi Department (December 1862-January 1863)
Cabell's Brigade, Steele's-Fagan's Division, District of Arkansas, Trans-Mississippi Department (April 1863-August 1864)
Cabell's Brigade, Fagan's Division, Price's Cavalry Corps (or Army of Missouri from September 18, 1864), Trans-Mississippi Department (August 1864-May 1865)
*Battles:* Cane Hill (November 28, 1862)
Prairie Grove (December 7, 1862)
Marmaduke's Expedition into Missouri (December 31, 1862-January 25, 1863)
Fayetteville (April 18, 1863)
Devil's Backbone (September 1, 1863)
Pine Bluff (October 25, 1863)
Camden Expedition (March-May 1864)
Poison Springs (April 18, 1864)
Marks' Mill (April 25, 1864)
Price's Missouri Raid (September-October 1864)

## 41. ARKANSAS 2ND CAVALRY BATTALION

*Organization:* Organized with five companies prior to February 23, 1862. Consolidated with the 6th (Phifer's) Cavalry Battalion and designated as the 2nd Cavalry Regiment at Corinth, Mississippi, on May 15, 1862.
*First Commander:* W. D. Barnett (Major)
*Assignments:* Hindman's Brigade, Hardee's Division, Central Army of Kentucky, Department #2 (February-March 1862)
Beall's Cavalry Brigade, Department #2 (April-May 1862)
*Battle:* Corinth Campaign (April-June 1862)

## 42. ARKANSAS 2ND CAVALRY BATTALION STATE TROOPS

*Organization:* Organized with an undetermined number of companies in late 1863. Increased to a regiment and designated as the 12th Cavalry Regiment on February 15, 1864.
*First Commander:* John C. Wright (Lieutenant Colonel)
*Field Officer:* James W. Bowie (Major)

## 43. ARKANSAS 2ND CAVALRY REGIMENT

*Also Known As:*  Arkansas 4th (Slemons') Cavalry Regiment

*Organization:*  Organized by the consolidation of the 2nd and 6th (Phifer's) Cavalry Battalions at Corinth, Mississippi, on May 15, 1862. Reduced to a battalion and designated as the 18th Cavalry Battalion ca. September 1864.

*First Commander:*  William F. Slemons (Colonel)

*Field Officers:*  Thomas M. Cochran (Lieutenant Colonel)
Thomas J. Reid, Jr. (Major)
William J. Somervell (Major)
H. R. Withers (Lieutenant Colonel)

*Assignments:*  Cavalry, 1st Corps, Army of the Mississippi, Department #2 (May-July 1862)

Armstrong's Cavalry Brigade, Price's Corps, Army of West Tennessee, Department #2 (July-October 1862)

Armstrong's Cavalry Brigade, Price's Corps, Army of West Tennessee, Department of Mississippi and East Louisiana (October-December 1862)

Jackson's Cavalry Corps, Army of North Mississippi, Department of Mississippi and East Louisiana (January 1862-January 1863)

Cavalry, Loring's Division, Army of North Mississippi, Department of Mississippi and East Louisiana (January-February 1863)

Slemons' Brigade, 5th Military District, Department of Mississippi and East Louisiana (May-September 1863)

Chalmers' Cavalry Brigade, Department of Mississippi and East Louisiana (September-October 1863)

Slemons' Brigade, Chalmers' Cavalry Division, Department of Mississippi and East Louisiana (October-November 1863)

Slemons' Brigade, Chalmers' Division, Lee's Cavalry Corps, Department of Mississippi and East Louisiana (November 1863-January 1864)

Slemons' Brigade, Chalmers' Division, Lee's Cavalry Corps, Department of Alabama, Mississippi and East Louisiana (January-March 1864)

Crawford's-Slemons' Brigade, Fagan's Cavalry Division, District of Arkansas, Trans-Mississippi Department (April-September 1864)

2nd (Slemons') Arkansas Cavalry Brigade, 1st (Fagan's) Arkansas Cavalry Division, Price's Cavalry Corps (or Army of Missouri from September 18, 1864), Trans-Mississippi Department (September 1864)

*Battles:*  Expedition from Holly Springs to Bolivar and Jackson, Tennessee (detachment) (July-August 1, 1862)

Iuka (September 19, 1862)

Corinth (October 3-4, 1862)

Yazoo Pass Expedition (February 3-April 10, 1863)

Charleston (March 13, 1863)

Austin, Mississippi (May 24, 1863)
near Commerce, Mississippi (June 17, 1863)
on the Coldwater River, Mississippi (June 19, 1863)
Camden Expedition (March-May 1864)
Poison Springs (April 18, 1864)
Marks' Mill (April 25, 1864)
Jenkins' Ferry (April 30, 1864)
**Further Reading:** Dupree, T.C., *The War-time Letters of Captain T.C. Dupree, C.S.A., 1864-1865.*

## 44.   ARKANSAS 2ND CAVALRY REGIMENT MOUNTED RIFLES

**Organization:** Organized and mustered in for one year on July 29, 1861. The "Texas Fencibles" were assigned as an unlettered company on August 13, 1861. Became Company A, 4th (Whitfield's) Cavalry Battalion, on November 12, 1861. Dismounted in April 1862. Reorganized on May 8, 1862. Consolidated with the 1st Mounted Rifled Regiment, 4th Infantry Battalion, 4th, 9th and 24th Infantry Regiments and designated as the 1st Mounted Rifles Regiment Consolidated at Smithfield, North Carolina, on April 9, 1865.
**First Commander:** James Q. McIntosh (Colonel)
**Field Officers:** Henry K. Brown (Major)
James P. Eagle (Major, Lieutenant Colonel)
Benjamin T. Embry (Lieutenant Colonel, Colonel)
Harris Flanagin (Colonel)
William Gipson (Major)
James T. Smith (Major, Lieutenant Colonel)
James A. Williamson (Lieutenant Colonel, Colonel)
**Assignments:** McCulloch's Brigade (August 1861)
Indian Territory (September-October 1861)
McCulloch's Division, Department #2 (October-December 1861)
McIntosh's Brigade, McCulloch's Division, Department #2 (December 1861-January 1862)
McIntosh's Brigade, McCulloch's Division, Trans-Mississippi District, Department #2 (January-March 1862)
Churchill's Cavalry Brigade, Price's Division, Trans-Mississippi District, Department #2 (March-April 1862)
Churchill's Brigade, McCown's Division, Army of the West, Department #2 (April-July 1862)
McNair's Brigade, McCown's Division, Department of East Tennessee (July-December 1862)
McNair's Brigade, McCown's Division, E. K. Smith's Corps, Army of Tennessee (December 1862-March 1863)

McNair's Brigade, McCown's Division, 1st Corps, Army of Tennessee (March-April 1863)

McNair's Brigade, Walker's Division, Department of the West (June 1863)

McNair's Brigade, French's Division, Department of the West (June-July 1863)

McNair's Brigade, French's Division, Department of Mississippi and East Louisiana (July-September 1863)

McNair's Brigade, Johnson's Provisional Division, Army of Tennessee (September 1863)

McNair's Brigade, French's Division, Department of Mississippi and East Louisiana (September 1863-January 1864)

McNair's Brigade, French's Division, Department of Alabama, Mississippi and East Louisiana (January-February 1864)

McNair's-D. H. Reynolds' Brigade, Department of the Gulf (February-April 1864)

D. H. Reynolds' Brigade, District of the Gulf, Department of Alabama, Mississippi and East Louisiana (April-May 1864)

D. H. Reynolds' Brigade, Cantey's-Walthall's Division, Army of Mississippi (May-July 1864)

D. H. Reynolds' Brigade, Walthall's Division, 3rd Corps, Army of Tennessee (July 1864-April 1865)

**Battles:** Wilson's Creek (August 10, 1861)
Chustenelah (December 26, 1861)
Pea Ridge (March 7-8, 1862)
Corinth Campaign (April-June 1862)
Farmington (May 9, 1862)
Richmond, Kentucky (August 29-30, 1862)
Perryville (October 8, 1862)
Murfreesboro (December 31, 1862-January 3, 1863)
Vicksburg Campaign (May-July 1863)
Jackson (May 14, 1863)
Jackson Siege (July 1863)
Chickamauga (September 19-20, 1863)
Chattanooga Siege (September-November 1863)
Atlanta Campaign (May-September 1864)
Dug Gap (May 8, 1864)
Resaca (May 14-15, 1864)
New Hope Church (May 25-June 4, 1864)
Pine Mountain (June 14, 1864)
Kennesaw Mountain (June 27, 1864)
Moore's Hill (July 19, 1864)
Peach Tree Creek (July 20, 1864)
Atlanta (July 22, 1864)

Ezra Church (July 28, 1864)
Atlanta Siege (July-September 1864)
Jonesboro (August 31-September 1, 1864)
Lovejoy's Station (September 2-5, 1864)
Moon's Station (October 4, 1864)
Franklin (November 30, 1864)
Nashville (December 15-16, 1864)
Sugar Creek (December 26, 1864)
Carolinas Campaign (February-April 1865)
Bentonville (March 19-21, 1865)
**Further Reading:** Leeper, Wesley Thurman, *Rebels Valiant, Second Mounted Rifles (Dismounted)*.

## 45. ARKANSAS 2ND (GORDON'S) CAVALRY REGIMENT
*See:* ARKANSAS 4TH (GORDON'S) CAVALRY REGIMENT

## 46. ARKANSAS 2ND (MORGAN'S) CAVALRY REGIMENT
**Organization:** Organized with 12 companies by the change of designation of the 5th Cavalry Regiment on December 24, 1863. Surrendered by General E. Kirby Smith, commanding the Trans-Mississippi Department, on May 26, 1865.
**First Commander:** Thomas J. Morgan (Colonel)
**Field Officers:** John P. Bull (Major, Lieutenant Colonel)
John W. Coarser (Lieutenant Colonel)
William N. Portis (Major)
**Assignments:** Cabell's Brigade, Marmaduke's Cavalry Division, District of
    Arkansas, Trans-Mississippi Department (December 1863-January 1864)
Cabell's Brigade, Fagan's Cavalry Division, District of Arkansas, Trans-Missis-
    sippi Department (April-August 1864)
1st (Cabell's) Arkansas Cavalry Brigade, 1st (Fagan's) Arkansas Cavalry Divi-
    sion, Price's Cavalry Corps (or Army of Missouri from September 18, 1864),
    Trans-Mississippi Department (August 1864-May 1865)
**Battles:** Camden Expedition (March-May 1864)
Poison Springs (April 18, 1864)
Marks' Mill (April 25, 1864)
Price's Missouri Raid (September-October 1864)
Marais des Cygnes (October 1864)

## 47. ARKANSAS 3RD CAVALRY REGIMENT
**Organization:** Organized with eight companies as the 1st Mounted Volunteers Regiment for one year on July 24, 1861. Mustered into state service at

Little Rock on June 10, 1861. Mustered into Confederate service on July 29, 1861. 1st Company E became Company E, 6th (Phifer's) Cavalry Battalion, in September 1861. Designated as the 3rd Cavalry Regiment on January 15, 1862. Dismounted at Des Arc in March 1862. Companies E, F and H, Williamson's Infantry Battalion, were assigned as Companies 2nd E, K and I, respectively, on May 25, 1862. Reorganized for two years on May 26, 1862. Remounted in November 1862. Surrendered by General Joseph E. Johnston at Durham Station, Orange County, North Carolina, on April 26, 1865.

**First Commander:**   Solon Borland (Colonel)

**Field Officers:**   William H. Blackwell (Major)
Benjamin F. Danley (Lieutenant Colonel)
Josiah F. Earle (Major)
Samuel G. Earle (Colonel)
James M. Gee (Lieutenant Colonel)
Marzarine J. Henderson (Major, Lieutenant Colonel)
Anson W. Hobson (Major, Colonel)
David F. Shall (Major)

**Assignments:**   District of Arkansas (July-September 1861)
District of Arkansas, Department #2 (September 1861-January 1862)
Roan's-Phifer's Brigade, Jones'-Maury's Division, Army of the West, Department #2 (April-July 1862)
Phifer's Brigade, Maury's Division, Price's Corps, Army of West Tennessee, Department #2 (July-October 1862)
Phifer's Brigade, Maury's Division, Price's Corps, Army of West Tennessee, Department of Mississippi and East Louisiana (October 1862)
Hébert's Brigade, Bowen's Division, Price's Corps, Army of West Tennessee, Department of Mississippi and East Louisiana (October 1862)
Cravens' Brigade, Bowen's Division, Price's Corps, Army of West Tennessee, Department of Mississippi and East Louisiana (October-December 1862)
2nd Brigade, Jackson's Division, Cavalry Corps, Department of Mississippi and East Louisiana (December 1862-February 1863)
Armstrong's Brigade, Jackson's Division, Cavalry Corps, Department of Mississippi and East Louisiana (February 1863)
Armstrong's Brigade, Jackson's Division, Van Dorn's Cavalry Corps, Army of Tennessee (February-May 1863)
Armstrong's Brigade, Forrest's Cavalry Division, Army of Tennessee (May-August 1863)
Armstrong's-Wheeler's Brigade, Armstrong's Division, Forrest's Cavalry Corps, Army of Tennessee (August-October 1863)
Harrison's Brigade, Wharton's Division, Wheeler's Cavalry Corps, Army of Tennessee (October-November 1863)

Harrison's Brigade, Wharton's Division, Martin's Cavalry Corps, Department of East Tennessee (November-December 1863)

Harrison's Brigade, Armstrong's Division, Martin's Cavalry Corps, Department of East Tennessee (December 1863-February 1864)

Harrison's Brigade, Humes' Division, Wheeler's Cavalry Corps, Army of Tennessee (April-October 1864)

Harrison's Brigade, Humes' Division, Wheeler's Cavalry Corps, Department of South Carolina, Georgia and Florida (October 1864-February 1865)

Harrison's Brigade, Humes' Division, Wheeler's Cavalry Corps, Hampton's Cavalry Command (February-April 1865)

Harrison's Brigade, Humes' Division, Wheeler's Cavalry Corps, Hampton's Cavalry Command, Army of Tennessee (April 1865)

**Battles:** Corinth Campaign (April-June 1862)

Corinth (October 3-4, 1862)

Holly Springs (December 20, 1862)

Thompson's Station (March 5, 1863)

Franklin (April 10, 1863)

Tullahoma Campaign (June 1863)

Chickamauga (September 19-20, 1863)

Chattanooga Siege (September-November 1863)

Knoxville Siege (November 1863)

Atlanta Campaign (May-September 1864)

Atlanta Siege (July-September 1864)

Flat Shoals (July 28, 1864)

Brown's Mill (July 30, 1864)

Strawberry Plains (August 24, 1864)

Thompson's Station (September 2, 1864)

Savannah Campaign (November-December 1864)

Carolinas Campaign (February-April 1865)

**Further Reading:** Collier, Calvin L., *The War Child's Children: The Story of the Third Regiment Arkansas Cavalry, C.S.A.*.

## 48.  ARKANSAS 4TH (GORDON'S) CAVALRY REGIMENT

**Also Known As:** Arkansas 2nd (Gordon's) Cavalry Regiment
Arkansas 9th Cavalry Regiment
Arkansas 11th Cavalry Regiment

**Organization:** Organized by the change of designation of the 1st (Carroll's-Thomson's) Cavalry Regiment on December 15, 1863. Surrendered by General E. Kirby Smith, commanding the Trans-Mississippi Department, on May 26, 1865.

**First Commander:** Anderson Gordon (Colonel)

*Field Officers:*   John A. Arrington (Major)
William A. Fayth (Major)
J. A. Johnson (Lieutenant Colonel)
*Assignments:*   Cabell's Brigade, Marmaduke's Cavalry Division, District of
   Arkansas, Trans-Mississippi Department (December 1863-January 1864)
Cabell's Brigade, Fagan's Cavalry Division, District of Arkansas, Trans-Missis-
   sippi Department (April-August 1864)
1st (Cabell's) Arkansas Cavalry Brigade, 1st (Fagan's) Arkansas Cavalry Bri-
   gade, Price's Cavalry Corps (or Army of Missouri from September 18, 1864),
   Trans-Mississippi Department (August 1864-May 1865)
*Battles:*   Camden Expedition (March-May 1864)
Poison Springs (April 18, 1864)
Marks' Mill (April 25, 1864)
Price's Missouri Raid (September-October 1864)

## 49.   ARKANSAS 4TH (SLEMONS') CAVALRY REGIMENT
*See:*   ARKANSAS 2ND CAVALRY REGIMENT

## 50.   ARKANSAS 5TH CAVALRY REGIMENT
*Organization:*   Organized with 12 companies ca. April 1863. Designation
changed to the 2nd (Morgan's) Cavalry Regiment on December 24, 1863.
*First Commander:*   Robert C. Newton (Colonel)
*Field Officers:*   John P. Bull (Lieutenant Colonel)
John Smith (Major)
*Assignments:*   Burbridge's Brigade, Marmaduke's Cavalry Division, District of
   Arkansas, Trans-Mississippi Department (May-June 1863)
Arkansas Cavalry Brigade, Walker's Cavalry Division, District of Arkansas,
   Trans-Mississippi Department (June-September 1863)
Dobbin's Cavalry Brigade, District of Arkansas, Trans-Mississippi Department
   (November-December 1863)
*Battles:*   Helena (July 4, 1863)
Little Rock (September 10, 1863)
Pine Bluff (October 25, 1863)

## 51.   ARKANSAS 6TH (PHIFER'S) CAVALRY BATTALION
*Also Known As:*   Arkansas 1st (Phifer's) Cavalry Battalion
*Organization:*   Organized with four Arkansas companies and two Louisiana
companies for the war ca. June 1861. Reduced to three companies ca. April 30,
1862. Consolidated with the 2nd Cavalry Battalion and designated as the 2nd
Cavalry Regiment at Corinth, Mississippi, on May 15, 1862.
*First Commander:*   Charles W. Phifer (Major)

*Field Officers:*   Archibald J. McNeill (Major)
David G. White (Major)

*Assignments:*   Cavalry, Hardee's Division, Central Army of Kentucky, Department #2 (October-November 1861)
Hindman's Brigade, Hardee's Division, Central Army of Kentucky, Department #2 (November 1861-March 1862)
Department #2 (March-May 1862)

*Battles:*   Brownsville, Kentucky (detachment) (November 20, 1861)
Rowlett's Station, Kentucky (December 17, 1861)

## 52.   ARKANSAS 6TH (FAGAN'S-MONROE'S) CAVALRY REGIMENT
*See:*   ARKANSAS 1ST (FAGAN'S-MONROE'S) CAVALRY REGIMENT

## 53.   ARKANSAS 7TH CAVALRY BATTALION
*See:*   ARKANSAS 7TH INFANTRY BATTALION

## 54.   ARKANSAS 7TH CAVALRY REGIMENT

*Organization:*   Organized by the increasing of Hill's Cavalry Battalion to a regiment on July 25, 1863. Surrendered by General E. Kirby Smith, commanding the Trans-Mississippi Department, on May 26, 1865.

*First Commander:*   John F. Hill (Colonel)

*Field Officers:*   James L. Adams (Major)
Oliver Basham (Lieutenant Colonel)
J. C. Ward (Major)

*Assignments:*   Cabell's Cavalry Brigade, District of the Indian Territory, Trans-Mississippi Department (July-November 1863)
Cabell's Brigade, Marmaduke's Cavalry Division, District of Arkansas, Trans-Mississippi Department (November 1863-January 1864)
Cabell's Brigade, Fagan's Cavalry Division, District of Arkansas, Trans-Mississippi Department (April-August 1864)
1st (Cabell's) Arkansas Cavalry Brigade, 1st (Fagan's) Arkansas Cavalry Division, Price's Cavalry Corps (or Army of Missouri from September 18, 1864) Trans-Mississippi Department (August 1864-May 1865)

*Battles:*   Devil's Backbone (September 1, 1863)
Camden Expedition (March-May 1864)
Poison Springs (April 18, 1864)
Marks' Mill (April 25, 1864)
Price's Missouri Raid (September-October 1864)
Marais des Cygnes (October 25, 1864)

## 55.   ARKANSAS 8TH CAVALRY REGIMENT
*See:*   ARKANSAS 2ND (MORGAN'S) CAVALRY REGIMENT

## 56.   ARKANSAS 9TH CAVALRY REGIMENT
*See:*   ARKANSAS 4TH (GORDON'S) CAVALRY REGIMENT

## 57.   ARKANSAS 10TH CAVALRY REGIMENT
*Organization:*   Organized by the mounting and consolidation of the 10th Infantry Regiment and remnants of other units in the summer of 1864. Surrendered by Brigadier General M. Jeff. Thompson, as part of the Army of the Northern Sub-district of Arkansas, District of Arkansas and West Louisiana, Trans-Mississippi Department, on May 11, 1865.
*First Commander:*   Allan R. Witt (Colonel)
*Assignments:*   Dobbin's Brigade, Fagan's Cavalry Division, District of Arkansas, Trans-Mississippi Department (August-September 1864)
Northern Sub-District of Arkansas, District of Arkansas, Trans-Mississippi Department (September 1864-April 1865)
Northern Sub-District of Arkansas, District of Arkansas and West Lousiana, Trans-Mississippi Department (April-May 1865)

## 58.   ARKANSAS 10TH (CRAWFORD'S) CAVALRY REGIMENT
*See:*   ARKANSAS 1ST (CRAWFORD'S) CAVALRY REGIMENT

## 59.   ARKANSAS 11TH CAVALRY REGIMENT
*See:*   ARKANSAS 4TH (GORDON'S) CAVALRY REGIMENT

## 60.   ARKANSAS 12TH CAVALRY REGIMENT
*Organization:*   Organized by the increasing of the 2nd Cavalry Battalion, State Troops, to a regiment on February 15, 1864. Surrendered by General E. Kirby Smith, commanding the Trans-Mississippi Department, on May 26, 1865.
*First Commander:*   John C. Wright (Colonel)
*Field Officers:*   James W. Bowie (Lieutenant Colonel)
George M. Wright (Major)
*Assignments:*   Crawford's-Slemons' Brigade, Fagan's Cavalry Division, District of Arkansas, Trans-Mississippi Department (April-September 1864)
2nd (Slemons'-Crawford's) Arkansas Cavalry Brigade, 1st (Fagan's) Arkansas Cavalry Division, Price's Cavalry Corps (or Army of Missouri from September 18, 1864), Trans-Mississippi Department (September 1864-May 1865)
*Battles:*   Camden Expedition (March-May 1864)

Poison Springs (April 18, 1864)
Marks' Mill (April 25, 1864)
Price's Missouri Raid (September-October 1864)

## 61. ARKANSAS 13TH CAVALRY BATTALION

*Also Known As:* Arkansas 16th Cavalry Battalion
*Organization:* Organized with four to six companies. Temporarily attached to the
1st (Fagan's-Monroe's) Cavalry Regiment in 1864. Surrendered by General E.
Kirby Smith, commanding the Trans-Mississippi Department, on May 26, 1865.
*First Commander:* James L. Witherspoon (Major)
*Field Officer:* James M. O'Neil (Major) (temporarily assigned from the 1st
[Fagan's-Monroe's] Cavalry Regiment)
*Assignments:* Cabell's Cavalry Brigade, District of the Indian Territory,
  Trans-Mississippi Department (July-November 1863)
Cabell's Brigade, Marmaduke's Cavalry Division, District of Arkansas, Trans-
  Mississippi Department (November 1863-January 1864)
Cabell's Brigade, Fagan's Cavalry Division, District of Arkansas, Trans-Missis-
  sippi Department (April-August 1864)
1st (Cabell's) Arkansas Cavalry Brigade, 1st (Fagan's) Arkansas Cavalry Divi-
  sion, Price's Cavalry Corps (or Army of Missouri from September 18, 1864)
  Trans-Mississippi Department (August 1864-May 1865)
*Battles:* Devil's Backbone (September 1, 1863)
Camden Expedition (March-May 1864)
Price's Missouri Raid (September-October 1864)

## 62. ARKANSAS 15TH CAVALRY BATTALION

*Organization:* Organized for service in the Indian Territory by the transfer of the
four Arkansas companies of Clark's Missouri Infantry Regiment on September
20, 1863, per S.O. #171, District of Arkansas, Trans-Mississippi Department.
Dismounted by order of Lieutenant General E. Kirby Smith, commanding the
Trans-Mississippi Department, on June 11, 1864. No further record.
*First Commander:* Michael W. Buster (Lieutenant Colonel)
*Assignment:* District of Arkansas Trans-Mississippi Department (September
1863-June 1864)

## 63. ARKANSAS 16TH CAVALRY BATTALION

*See:* ARKANSAS 13TH CAVALRY BATTALION

## 64. ARKANSAS 17TH CAVALRY BATTALION

*Organization:* Organized with five to seven companies by the change of
designation of Crawford's Cavalry Battalion on April 20, 1864. Surrendered by

General E. Kirby Smith, commanding the Trans-Mississippi Department, on
May 26, 1865.

**First Commander:**  John M. Harrell (Lieutenant Colonel)

**Field Officer:**  J. W. Bishop (Major)

**Assignments:**  Cabell's Brigade, Fagan's Cavalry Division, District of Arkansas, Trans-Mississippi Department (April-August 1864)

1st (Cabell's) Arkansas Cavalry Brigade, 1st (Fagan's) Arkansas Cavalry Division, Price's Cavalry Corps (or Army of Missouri from September 18, 1864) Trans-Mississippi Department (August 1864-May 1865)

**Battles:**  Camden Expedition (March-May 1864)

Marks' Mill (April 25, 1864)

Price's Missouri Raid (September-October 1864)


## 65.  ARKANSAS 18TH CAVALRY BATTALION

**Organization:**  Organized by the reduction of the 2nd Cavalry Regiment to a battalion ca. September 1864. Surrendered by General E. Kirby Smith, commanding the Trans-Mississippi Department, on May 26, 1865.

**First Commander:**  Elisha L. McMurtrey (Lieutenant Colonel)

**Assignment:**  2nd (Slemon's-Crawford's) Arkansas Cavalry Brigade, 1st (Fagan's) Arkansas Cavalry Division, Price's Cavalry Corps (or Army of Missouri from September 18, 1864), Trans-Mississippi Department (September-October 1864)

**Battles:**  Price's Missouri Raid (September-October 1864)

Pilot Knob (September 27, 1864)

Independence (October 22, 1864)

Marais des Cygnes (October 25, 1864)


## 66.  ARKANSAS ANDERSON'S CAVALRY BATTALION

**Organization:**  Organized with four companies in the summer of 1864. No record after September 18, 1864.

**First Commander:**  William L. Anderson (Captain)

**Assignment:**  Unattached, Fagan's Cavalry Division, Price's Cavalry Corps (or Army of Missouri from September 18, 1864), Trans-Mississippi Department (August-September 1864)

**Battle:**  Price's Missouri Raid (September-October 1864)


## 67.  ARKANSAS CARLTON'S CAVALRY BATTALION

**Organization:**  Organized in summer of 1864. No record after September 1864.

**First Commander:**  Charles H. Carlton (Colonel)

**Field Officers:**  D. J. Peoples (Major)

R. H. Thompson (Lieutenant Colonel)

**Assignment:** Slemons' Brigade, Fagan's Cavalry Division, Price's Cavalry Corps (or Army of Missouri from September 18, 1864), Trans-Mississippi Department (August-September 1864)

**Battle:** Price's Missouri Raid (September-October 1864)

## 68. ARKANSAS CHRISMAN'S CAVALRY BATTALION

**Organization:** Organized with four companies on September 28, 1862. Increased to a regiment and designated as the 1st (Dobbin's) Cavalry Regiment in early 1863.

**First Commander:** Francis M. Chrisman (Major)

**Assignments:** Parson's Cavalry Brigade, 1st Corps, Army of the West, Trans-Mississippi Department (September 1862)

Unattached, District of Arkansas, Trans-Mississippi Department (December 1862-January 1863)

## 69. ARKANSAS CRAWFORD'S CAVALRY BATTALION

**Organization:** Organized with five to seven companies ca. March 1863. Became the 17th Cavalry Battalion on April 20, 1864.

**First Commander:** William A. Crawford (Lieutenant Colonel)

**Assignments:** Cabell's Cavalry Brigade, District of the Indian Territory, Trans-Mississippi Department (June-November 1863)

Cabell's Brigade, Marmaduke's Cavalry Division, District of Arkansas, Trans-Mississippi Department (December 1863-January 1864)

Cabell's Brigade, Fagan's Cavalry Division, District of Arkansas, Trans-Mississippi Department (April 1864)

**Battles:** Devil's Backbone (September 1, 1863)

Camden Expedition (March-May 1864)

## 70. ARKANSAS DAVIES' CAVALRY BATTALION

**Organization:** Organized with at least five companies. Not listed in the *Official Records.* Surrendered by Brigadier General M. Jeff. Thompson, commanding the Army of the Northern Sub-district of Arkansas, District of Arkansas and West Louisiana, Trans-Mississippi Department, on May 11, 1865.

**First Commander:** Davies

**Assignments:** Northern Sub-district of Arkansas, District of Arkansas, Trans-Mississippi Department (April 1865)

Northern Sub-district of Arkansas, District of Arkansas and West Louisiana, Trans-Mississippi Department (April-May 1865)

## 71. ARKANSAS FORD'S CAVALRY BATTALION

*Organization:* Organized with an undetermined number of companies on August 27, 1864. No record after December 1864.
*First Commander:* Barney Ford (Lieutenant Colonel)
*Field Officer:* E. O. Wolf (Major)
*Assignment:* Freeman's Brigade, Marmaduke's Division, Price's Cavalry Corps (or Army of Missouri from September 18, 1864), Trans-Mississippi Department (August-September 1864)
*Battle:* Price's Missouri Raid (September-October 1864)

## 72. ARKANSAS GIPSON'S CAVALRY REGIMENT MOUNTED RIFLES

*Organization:* Organized with nine companies early in the war. Unit not listed in the *Official Records.* At least two companies assigned to the 1st (Carroll's-Thompson's) Cavalry Regiment.
*First Commander:* William Gipson (Major)

## 73. ARKANSAS GUNTER'S CAVALRY BATTALION

*Organization:* Organized with an undetermined number of companies by April 20, 1864. Surrendered by General E. Kirby Smith, commanding the Trans-Mississippi Department, on May 26, 1865.
*First Commander:* Thomas M. Gunter (Lieutenant Colonel)
*Field Officer:* James Woosley (Major)
*Assignments:* Cabell's Brigade, Fagan's Cavalry Division, District of Arkansas, Trans-Mississippi Department (April-August 1864)
1st (Cabell's) Arkansas Cavalry Brigade, 1st (Fagan's) Cavalry Division, Price's Cavalry Corps (or Army of Missouri from September 18, 1864), Trans-Mississippi Department (August 1864-May 1865)
*Battles:* Devil's Backbone (September 1, 1863)
Camden Expedition (March-May 1864)
Poison Springs (April 18, 1864)
Marks' Mill (April 25, 1864)
Price's Missouri Raid (September-October 1864)

## 74. ARKANSAS HILL'S CAVALRY BATTALION

*Organization:* Organized with an undetermined number of companies ca. April 1863. Increased to a regiment and designated as the 7th Cavalry Regiment on July 25, 1863.
*First Commander:* John F. Hill (Lieutenant Colonel)
*Assignments:* Cabell's Cavalry Brigade, District of Arkansas, Trans-Mississippi Department (April 1863)

Cabell's Cavalry Brigade, District of the Indian Territory, Trans-Mississippi Department (April-July 1863)

## 75. ARKANSAS JOHNSON'S CAVALRY BATTALION

*Organization:* Apparently organized in 1862. Not listed at the National Archives. Does not appear in the *Official Records.* Increased to a regiment and designated as the 1st (Fagan's-Monroe's) Cavalry Regiment in late 1862.
*First Commander:* A. H. Johnson (Major)

## 76. ARKANSAS MCGEHEE'S CAVALRY REGIMENT

*Also Known As:* McGehee's Mounted Infantry Regiment
*Organization:* Organized in the summer of 1864. Surrendered by Brigadier General M. Jeff. Thompson, commanding the Army of the Northern Sub-district of Arkansas, District of Arkansas and West Louisiana, Trans-Mississippi Department, on May 11, 1865.
*First Commander:* James H. McGehee (Colonel)
*Field Officer:* Jesse S. Grider (Lieutenant Colonel)
*Assignments:* Dobbin's Brigade, Fagan's Cavalry Division, District of Arkansas, Trans-Mississippi Department (August-September 1864)
Northern Sub-District of Arkansas, District of Arkansas, Trans-Mississippi Department (April 1865)
Northern Sub-District of Arkansas, District of Arkansas and West Lousiana, Trans-Mississippi Department (April-May 1865)

## 77. ARKANSAS MATLOCK'S CAVALRY BATTALION

*Also Known As:* Matlock's Cavalry Regiment
*Organization:* Organized on June 16, 1862. Dismounted on July 18, 1862. Increased to a regiment and designated as the 32nd Infantry Regiment on August 6, 1862.
*First Commander:* Charles H. Matlock (Lieutenant Colonel)

## 78. ARKANSAS NAVE'S CAVALRY BATTALION

*Organization:* Organized with about five companies at an undetermined date. Not listed in the *Official Records.* Surrendered by Brigadier General M. Jeff. Thompson, as part of the Army of the Northern Sub-district of Arkansas, District of Arkansas, Trans-Mississippi Department, on May 11, 1865.
*First Commander:* R. H. Nave (Major)
*Assignments:* Northern Sub-District of Arkansas, District of Arkansas, Trans-Mississippi Department (April 1865)
Northern Sub-District of Arkansas, District of Arkansas and West Lousiana, Trans-Mississippi Department (April-May 1865)

## 79. ARKANSAS POE'S CAVALRY BATTALION

*Organization:* Organized with two companies from the remnants of the 11th Infantry Regiment Mounted and other units that had become scattered after the fall of Port Hudson, Louisiana, on July 8, 1863. Apparently a temporary field organization. One company transferred to the 1st (Crawford's) Cavalry Regiment as Company M. No record after the summer of 1864.

*First Commander:* James T. Poe (Major)

*Assignment:* Crawford's Brigade, Fagan's Cavalry Division, District of Arkansas, Trans-Mississippi Department (April-July 1864)

## 80. ARKANSAS ROBERTSON'S CAVALRY SQUADRON

*Organization:* Date of organization with two companies is undetermined. Unit not listed at the National Archives or in the *Official Records.*

*First Commander:* J. L. Robertson (Major)

# INFANTRY

## 81. ARKANSAS 1ST INFANTRY BATTALION

*Organization:* Organized with eight companies (lettered from L to P and R to T) as an extra force attached to the 2nd Infantry Regiment at some time prior to August 1861. Two additional unlettered companies attached, and it was redesignated as the 18th (Marmaduke's) Infantry Regiment in December 1861.

*First Commander:* Jonathan S. Marmaduke (Lieutenant Colonel)

*Field Officer:* James B. Johnson (Major)

*Assignments:* Upper District of Arkansas (August-September 1861)

Indian Territory (September-October 1861)

Hindman's Brigade, Hardee's Division, Central Army of Kentucky, Department #2 (October-December 1861)

*Battle:* Rowlett's Station, Kentucky (December 17, 1861)

## 82. ARKANSAS 1ST (JONES') INFANTRY BATTALION

*See:* ARKANSAS 8TH INFANTRY BATTALION

## 83. ARKANSAS 1ST INFANTRY REGIMENT

*Organization:* Organized at Little Rock in May 1861. Mustered into Confederate service for 12 months by companies at Lynchburg, Virginia, on May 9-21, 1861. Fagan Rifles assigned as an unlettered company on October 12, 1861. It later became Company C, 2nd Infantry Battalion. Reorganized for the war in the spring of 1862. Field consolidation with the 15th Infantry Regiment from the spring of 1864 to early 1865. Additional field consolidation with the 2nd, 5th, 13th and 24th Infantry Regiments and the 3rd Confederate Infantry Regiment from December 1864 to March 1865. 15th and 24th Infantry Regiments and the 3rd Confederate Infantry Regiment detached from this field consolidation in early 1865. Consolidated with the 2nd, 5th, 6th, 7th, 8th, 13th, 15th, 19th (Dawson's) and 24th Infantry Regiments and the 3rd Confederate Infantry Regiment and designated as the 1st Infantry Regiment Consolidated at Smithfield, North Carolina, on April 9, 1865.

*First Commander:*  James F. Fagan (Colonel)

*Field Officers:*  John W. Colquitt (Major, Colonel)
William A. Crawford (Lieutenant Colonel)
Atkinson Little (Major)
William H. Martin (Major, Lieutenant Colonel)
Donelson McGregor (Lieutenant Colonel)
James C. Monroe (Lieutenant Colonel)
John B. Thompson (Major, Lieutenant Colonel)

*Assignments:*  Department of Fredericksburg (July-September 1861)
Walker's Brigade, Department of Fredericksburg (September-October 1861)
Walker's Brigade, Aquia District, Department of Northern Virginia (October 1861-January 1862)
Gibson's Brigade, Ruggles' Division, 2nd Corps, Army of the Mississippi, Department #2 (March-April 1862)
Moore's Brigade, Ruggles' Division, 2nd Corps, Army of the Mississippi, Department #2 (April-May 1862)
L. M. Walker's Brigade, Anderson's Division, 2nd Corps, Army of the Mississippi, Department #2 (June-July 1862)
L. M. Walker's Brigade, Jones' Division, Army of the Mississippi, Department #2 (July-August 1862)
Powel's Brigade, Anderson's Division, Left Wing, Army of the Mississippi, Department #2 (August-November 1862)
Powel's Brigade, Anderson's Division, 2nd Corps, Army of Tennessee, (November-December 1862)
Polk's Brigade, Cleburne's Division, 1st Corps, Army of Tennessee (December 1862-July 1864)
Govan's Brigade, Cleburne's Division, 1st Corps, Army of Tennessee (July 1864-April 1865)

*Battles:*  1st Bull Run (July 21, 1861)
Shiloh (April 6-7, 1862)
Perryville October 8, 1862
Murfreesboro (December 31, 1862-January 3, 1863)
Tullahoma Campaign (June 1863)
Chickamauga (September 19-20, 1863)
Chattanooga Siege (September-November 1863)
Chattanooga (November 23-25, 1863)
Atlanta Campaign (May-September 1864)
New Hope Church (May 25-June 4, 1864)
Kennesaw Mountain (June 27, 1864)

Atlanta (July 22, 1864)
Atlanta Siege (July-September 1864)
Jonesboro (August 31-September 1, 1864)
Franklin (November 30, 1864)
Nashville (December 15-16, 1864)
Carolinas Campaign (February-April 1865)
Bentonville (March 19-21, 1865)
**Further Reading:** Bevens, W. E., *Reminiscences of a Private, Company G. First Arkansas Regiment Infantry*. Hammock, John C., *With Honor Untarnished, the Story of the First Arkansas Infantry Regiment, Confederate States Army*.

## 84. ARKANSAS 1ST INFANTRY REGIMENT CONSOLIDATED

**Organization:** Organized by the consolidation of the 1st, 2nd, 5th, 8th, 13th, 15th, 19th (Dawson's) and 24th Infantry Regiments and the 3rd Infantry Regiment at Smithfield, North Carolina, on April 9, 1865. Surrendered by General Joseph E. Johnston at Durham Station, Orange County, North Carolina, on April 26, 1865.
**First Commander:** E. A. Howell (Colonel)
**Assignment:** Govan's Brigade, Brown's Division, 1st Corps, Army of Tennessee (April 1865)
**Battle:** Carolinas Campaign (February-April 1865)

## 85. ARKANSAS 1ST INFANTRY REGIMENT CONSOLIDATED TRANS-MISSISSIPPI DEPARTMENT

**Organization:** Organized with 10 numbered companies by the consolidation of the 14th (Mitchell's-Powers'), 15th Northwest, 16th and 21st Infantry Regiments in January 1864. Surrendered by General E. Kirby Smith, commanding the Trans-Mississippi Department, on May 26, 1865.
**First Commander:** Jordan E. Cravens (Colonel)
**Assignment:** 2nd (McNair's) Arkansas Brigade, 1st (Churchill's) Arkansas Division, 2nd Corps, Trans-Mississippi Department (September 1864-May 1865)

## 86. ARKANSAS 1ST INFANTRY REGIMENT STATE TROOPS

**Organization:** Organized at Mound City, Tennessee, on May 14, 1861. Transferred to Confederate service on July 23, 1861. Designated as the 15th Infantry Regiment by the War Department on December 31, 1861.
**First Commander:** Patrick R. Cleburne (Colonel)
**Field Officers:** John E. Glenn (Major)
James T. Harris (Major)
Archibald K. Patton (Lieutenant Colonel)

*Assignment:*  Upper District of Arkansas (June-July 1861)

## 87.  ARKANSAS 1ST INFANTRY REGIMENT VOLUNTEERS (MILITIA)

*Organization:*  Mustered into Confederate service by companies for 30 days between November 15 and 19, 1861. Mustered out by companies between December 15 and 19, 1861.
*First Commander:*  James H. McCaleb (Colonel)
*Field Officers:*  John Black (Major)
Liggin (Lieutenant Colonel)

## 88.  ARKANSAS 1ST (CLEBURNE'S) INFANTRY REGIMENT

*See:*  ARKANSAS 15TH INFANTRY REGIMENT

## 89.  ARKANSAS 1ST (RECTOR'S) INFANTRY REGIMENT NORTHWEST DIVISION

*See:*  ARKANSAS 35TH INFANTRY REGIMENT

## 90.  ARKANSAS 1ST TRANS-MISSISSIPPI INFANTRY REGIMENT

*See:*  ARKANSAS 37TH INFANTRY REGIMENT

## 91.  ARKANSAS 2ND INFANTRY BATTALION

*Organization:*  Mustered in as independent companies between September 29 and October 11, 1861. Organized with three companies on October 29, 1861, per S.O. #173, Aquia District, Department of Northern Virginia. Reorganized in the spring of 1862. Maryland Zouaves attached from February 1862 to June 1862. Permanently attached to the 3rd Infantry Regiment on July 25, 1862, per S.O. #152, Department of Northern Virginia.
*First Commander:*  William N. Bronaugh (Major)
*Assignments:*  French's Brigade, Aquia District, Department of Northern Virginia (January-March 1862)
Pettigrew's Brigade, Whiting's-G. W. Smith's-Whiting's Division, Army of Northern Virginia (March-June 1862)
Pender's Brigade, A. P. Hill's Division, Army of Northern Virginia (June 1862)
Pender's Brigade, A. P. Hill's Division, 1st Corps, Army of Northern Virginia (June-July 1862)
Walker's Brigade, Department of North Carolina (July 1862)
*Battles:*  Yorktown Siege (April-May 1862)
Seven Pines (May 31-June 1, 1862)
Seven Days Battles (June 25-July 1, 1862)

## 92. ARKANSAS 2ND INFANTRY REGIMENT

*Organization:* Organized in the spring of 1861, Mustered into Confederate service by companies between May 26 and June 26, 1861. Portion of 11th Infantry Regiment not captured at Island #10 served as 2nd Company E from May 25, 1862, to September 1862. Field consolidation with the 15th Infantry Regiment from the summer of 1863 to early 1864. Additional field consolidation with the 24th Infantry Regiment from November 16, 1863, to early 1865. Additional field consolidation with the 1st, 5th, 13th and 15th Infantry Regiments and the 3rd Confederate Infantry Regiment from December 1864 to early 1865. New field consolidation with the 1st, 5th and 13th Infantry Regiments in early 1865. Consolidated with the 1st, 5th, 6th, 7th, 8th, 13th, 15th, 19th (Dawson's) and 24th Infantry Regiments and the 3rd Confederate Infantry Regiment and designated as the 1st Infantry Regiment Consolidated at Smithfield, North Carolina, on April 9, 1865.

*First Commander:* Thomas G. Hindman (Colonel)
*Field Officers:* Joseph W. Bocage (Lieutenant Colonel)
Eldridge G. Brasher (Major, Lieutenant Colonel)
Daniel C. Govan (Lieutenant Colonel, Colonel)
Reuben F. Harvey (Major, Lieutenant Colonel)
A. T. Meek (Major)
James W. Scaife (Major, Lieutenant Colonel, Colonel)
Elisha Warfield (Major, Lieutenant Colonel, Colonel)

*Assignments:* Upper District of Arkansas (August 1861-September 1861)
Indian Territory (September-October 1861)
Hindman's Brigade, Hardee's Division, Central Army of Kentucky, Department #2 (October 1861-March 1862)
Hindman's Brigade, 3rd Corps, Army of the Mississippi, Department #2 (March-July 1862)
Hindman's-Liddell's Brigade, Buckner's DIvision, Army of the Mississippi, Department #2 (July-August 1862)
Liddell's Brigade, Buckner's Division, Left Wing, Army of the Mississippi, Department #2 (August-November 1862)
Liddell's Brigade, Buckner's-Cleburne's Division, 2nd Corps, Army of Tennessee (November 1862-September 1863)
Liddell's Brigade, Liddell's Division, Reserve Corps, Army of Tennessee (September 1863)
Liddell's Brigade, Cleburne's Division, 2nd Corps, Army of Tennessee (October-November 1863)
Liddell's-Govan's Brigade, Cleburne's-Brown's Division, 1st Corps, Army of Tennessee (November 1863-April 1865)

*Battles:* Rowlett's Station, Kentucky (December 17, 1861)

Shiloh (April 6-7, 1862)
Corinth Campaign (April 1862-June 1862)
Richmond, Kentucky (August 29-30, 1862)
Perryville (October 8, 1862)
Murfreesboro (December 31, 1862-January 3, 1983)
Tullahoma Campaign (June 1863)
Liberty Gap (June 24-26, 1863)
Chickamauga (September 19-20, 1863)
Chattanooga Siege (September-November 1863)
Chattanooga (November 23-25, 1863)
Ringgold Gap (November 27, 1863)
Atlanta Campaign (May-September 1864)
Dalton (May 5-11, 1864)
Resaca (May 14-15, 1864)
New Hope Church (May 25-June 4, 1864)
Kennesaw Mountain (June 27, 1864)
Peach Tree Creek (July 20, 1864)
Atlanta (July 22, 1864)
Jonesboro (August 31-September 1, 1864)
Franklin (November 30, 1864)
Nashville (December 15-16, 1864)
Carolinas Campaign (February-April 1865)
Bentonville (March 19-21, 1865)

## 93.  ARKANSAS 2ND INFANTRY REGIMENT CONSOLIDATED TRANS-MISSISSIPPI DEPARTMENT

**Organization:**  Organized with 10 numbered companies by the consolidation of the 12th Infantry Regiment with other units prior to September 30, 1864. Surrendered by General E. Kirby Smith, commanding the Trans-Mississippi Department, on May 26, 1865.

**First Commander:**  Thomas J. Reid, Jr. (Colonel)

**Assignment:**  2nd (McNair's) Arkansas Brigade, 1st (Churchill's) Arkansas Division, 2nd Corps, Trans-Mississippi Department (September 1864-May 1865)

## 94.  ARKANSAS 1ST INFANTRY REGIMENT VOLUNTEERS

**Organization:**  Organized with four companies of the 1st Battalion (a militia unit that is not mentioned in the *Official Records*) for 30 days in November 1861. Mustered into Confederate service by companies for 30 days between November 18 and 24, 1861. Mustered out on December 18, 1861.

## 95.  ARKANSAS 2ND (BROOKS') INFANTRY REGIMENT
*See:*  ARKANSAS 34TH INFANTRY REGIMENT

## 96.  ARKANSAS 2ND TRANS-MISSISSIPPI INFANTRY REGIMENT
*See:*  ARKANSAS 36TH INFANTRY REGIMENT

## 97.  ARKANSAS 3RD INFANTRY BATTALION
*Organization:*  Organized with seven companies on July 15, 1861. Increased to a regiment and designated as the 21st (McRae's) Infantry Regiment on December 3, 1861.
*First Commander:*  Dandridge McRae (Lieutenant Colonel)
*Field Officer:*  Thomas H. McRay (Major)
*Assignments:*  McCulloch's Brigade (August 1861)
Indian Territory (August-September 1861)
McCulloch's Division, Department #2 (October-December 1861)
*Battle:*  Wilson's Creek (August 10, 1861)

## 98.  ARKANSAS 3RD INFANTRY REGIMENT
*Organization:*  Organized on July 5, 1861. Mustered into Confederate service for the war in June or July 1861. Surrendered at Appomattox Court House, Virginia, on April 9, 1865.
*First Commander:*  Albert Rust (Colonel)
*Field Officers:*  Seth M. Barton (Lieutenant Colonel)
J. Hickson Capers (Major)
Van(noy) H. Manning (Major, Lieutenant Colonel)
John W. Ready (Major)
Samuel W. Smith (Major)
Robert S. Taylor (Major, Lieutenant Colonel)
William H. Tebbs (Lieutenant Colonel)
William K. Wilkins (Major)
*Assignments:*  Army of the Northwest (July 1861)
Jackson's Brigade, Army of the Northwest (September-October 1861)
Taliaferro's Brigade, Army of the Northwest (November 1861-February 1862)
Walker's Brigade, Aquia District, Department of Northern Virginia (February-March 1862)
Walker's Brigade, Department of North Carolina (March-August 1862)
Walker's-Cook's Brigade, Walker's-Ransom's Division, 1st Corps, Army of Northern Virginia (September-November 1862)
Texas Brigade, Hood's Division, 1st Corps, Army of Northern Virginia (November 1862-February 1863)

Texas Brigade, Hood's Division, Department of North Carolina and Southern Virginia (February-April 1863)

Texas Brigade, Hood's Division, Department of Southern Virginia (April-May 1863)

Texas Brigade, Hood's Division, 1st Corps, Army of Northern Virginia (May-September 1863)

Texas Brigade, Hood's Division, Longstreet's Corps, Army of Tennessee (September-November 1863)

Texas Brigade, Hood's-Field's Division, Department of East Tennessee (November 1863-April 1864)

Texas Brigade, Field's Division, Army of Northern Virginia (April 1864-April 1865)

**Battles:**   Greenbrier River (October 3, 1861)

Cheat Mountain (September 1862)

Romney Campaign (January 1862)

Seven Days Battles (June 25-July 1, 1862)

Malvern Cliff (June 30, 1862)

Harpers Ferry (September 12-15, 1862)

Antietam (September 17, 1862)

Fredericksburg (December 13, 1862)

Washington, North Carolina (March 30-April 14, 1863)

Suffolk Campaign (April-May 1863)

Gettysburg (July 1-3, 1863)

Chickamauga (September (19-20, 1863)

Chattanooga Siege (September-November 1863)

Wauhatchie (October 28-29, 1863)

Knoxville Siege (November 1863)

The Wilderness (May 5-6, 1864)

Spotsylvania Court House (May 8-21, 1864)

North Anna (May 23-26, 1864)

Cold Harbor (June 1-3, 1864)

Petersburg Siege (June 1864-April 1865)

3rd New Market Heights (September 29, 1864)

Chaffin's Farm (September 29, 1864)

Fort Gilmer (September 29-30, 1864)

Appomattox Court House (April 9, 1865)

**Further Reading:**   Collier, Calvin L., *"They'll do to tie to!": The Story of the Third Regiment, Arkansas Infantry, C.S.A.*

## 99.   ARKANSAS 3RD INFANTRY REGIMENT CONSOLIDATED TRANS-MISSISSIPPI DEPARTMENT

**Organization:**  Organized by the consolidation of the 15th (Gee's-Johnson's), 20th and Dawson's-Hardy's Consolidated Infantry Regiments on November 29,

1864. There is some evidence that it was already organized prior to September 20, 1864.

*First Commander:* H. G. P. Williamson (Colonel)

*Assignment:* 2nd (McNair's) Arkansas Brigade, 1st (Churchill's) Arkansas Division, 2nd Corps, Trans-Mississippi Department (September 1864-May 1865)

## 100. ARKANSAS 3RD INFANTRY REGIMENT STATE TROOPS

*Organization:* Organized in June 1861. Mustered out in September 1861.

*First Commander:* Jonathan R. Gratiot (Colonel)

*Field Officers:* David Provence (Lieutenant Colonel)

H. Ward (Major)

*Assignment:* Pearce's Arkansas State Troops Brigade (June-September 1861)

*Battle:* Wilson's Creek (August 10, 1861)

## 101. ARKANSAS 3RD TRANS-MISSISSIPPI INFANTRY REGIMENT

*See:* ARKANSAS 26TH INFANTRY REGIMENT

## 102. ARKANSAS 4Th INFANTRY BATTALION

*Organization:* Organized with five companies on November 30, 1861. Company D became Company H., 1st Tennessee Heavy Artillery. Field consolidation with the 4th and 31st Infantry Regiments from the summer of 1863 to 1864. Apparently consolidated with the 4th, 9th and 25th Infantry Regiments and the 1st and 2nd Mounted Rifles Regiments and designated as the 1st Mounted Rifles Consolidated Regiment at Smithfield, North Carolina, on April 9, 1865.

*First Commander:* Francis A. Terry (Lieutenant Colonel)

*Field Officers:* John McKay (Major)

Jesse A. Ross (Major)

*Assignments:* Stewart's Brigade, 1st Geographical Division, Department #2 (January-February 1862)

Stewart's Brigade, McCown's Command, 1st Geographical Division, Department #2 (February-April 1862)

Churchill's Brigade, McCown's Division, Army of the West, Department #2 (June-July 1862)

McNair's Brigade, McCown's Division, Department of East Tennessee (July-August 1862)

McNair's Brigade, McCown's Division, Army of Kentucky, Department #2 (August-October 1862)

McNair's Brigade, McCown's Division, Smith's Corps, Army of Tennessee (November 1862-March 1863)

McNair's Brigade, Stewart's Division, 1st Corps, Army of Tennessee (March-April 1863 )

McNair's Brigade, Walker's Division, Department of the West (June 1863)

McNair's Brigade, French's Division, Department of the West (June-July 1863)

McNair's Brigade, French's Division, Department of Mississippi and East Louisiana (July-August 1863)

McNair's Brigade, Johnson's Provisional Division, Army of Tennessee (September 1863)

McNair's Brigade, French's Division, Department of Mississippi and East Louisiana (September 1863-January 1864)

McNair's Brigade, French's Division, Department of Alabama, Mississippi and East Louisiana (January-February 1864)

McNair's-D. H. Reynold's Brigade, Department of the Gulf (February-April 1864)

D. H. Reynold's Brigade, District of the Gulf, Department of Alabama, Mississippi and East Louisiana (April-May 1864)

D. H. Reynold's Brigade, Cantey's-Walhall's Division, Army of Mississippi (May-July 1864)

D. H. Reynolds' Brigade, Walthall's Division, 3rd Corps, Army of Tennessee (July 1864-April 1865)

**Battles:**   Island #10 (April 6-7, 1862)
Corinth Campaign (April-June 1862)
Richmond, Kentucky (August 29-30, 1862)
Murfreesboro (December 31, 1862-January 3, 1863)
Jackson Siege (July 1863)
Chickamauga (September 19-20, 1863)
Chattanooga Siege (September-November 1863)
Atlanta Campaign (May-September 1864)
Dug Gap (May 8, 1864)
Resaca (May 14-15, 1864)
New Hope Church (May 25-June 4, 1864)
Kennesaw Mountain (June 27, 1864)
Peach Tree Creek (July 20, 1864)
Atlanta (July 22, 1864)
Ezra Church (July 28, 1864)
Atlanta Siege (July-September 1864)
Jonesboro (August 31-September 1, 1864)
Lovejoy's Station (September 2-5, 1864)
Franklin (November 30, 1864)
Nashville (December 15-16, 1864)
Sugar Creek (December 26, 1864)

Carolinas Campaign (February-April 1865)
Bentonville (March 19-21, 1865)

## 103. ARKANSAS 4TH INFANTRY REGIMENT

*Organization:* Organized and mustered into Confederate service at Miller's Springs, Lawrence County, Missouri, on August 17, 1861. 11th unlettered company mustered in on November 11, 1861. Became Company H, 16th Infantry Regiment, on December 4, 1861. Reorganized at Corinth, Mississippi, on May 8, 1862. Consolidated with the 1st and 2nd Mounted Rifles Regiments, 4th Infantry Battalion and 9th and 25th Infantry Regiments and designated as the 1st Mounted Rifles Regiment Consolidated at Smithfield, North Carolina, on April 9, 1865.

*First Commander:* Evander McNair (Colonel)

*Field Officers:* Henry G. Bunn (Lieutenant Colonel, Colonel)
James H. May (Major, Lieutenant Colonel)
Joseph B. McCulloch (Major)
Samuel Ogden (Lieutenant Colonel)

*Assignments:* McCulloch's Brigade (August 1861)
Indian Territory (September-October 1861)
McCulloch's Division, Department #2 (October-December 1861)
McIntosh's Brigade, McCulloch's Division, Department #2 (December 1861-January 1862)
McIntosh's Brigade, McCulloch's Division, Trans-Mississippi District, Department #2 (January-March 1862)
Churchill's Cavalry Brigade, Price's Division, Trans-Mississippi District, Department #2 (March-April 1862)
Churchill's Brigade, McCown's Division, Army of the West, Department #2 (April-July 1862)
McNair's Brigade, McCown's Division, Department of East Tennessee (July-December 1862)
McNair's Brigade, McCown's Division, E. K. Smith's Corps, Army of Tennessee (December 1862-March 1863)
McNair's Brigade, McCown's Division, 1st Corps, Army of Tennessee (March-April 1863)
McNair's Brigade, Walker's Division, Department of the West (June 1863)
McNair's Brigade, French's Division, Department of the West (June-July 1863)
McNair's Brigade, French's Division, Department of Mississippi and East Louisiana (July-September 1863)
McNair's Brigade, Johnson's Provisional Division, Army of Tennessee (September 1863)

McNair's Brigade, French's Division, Department of Mississippi and East Louisiana (September 1863-January 1864)

McNair's Brigade, French's Division, Department of Alabama, Mississippi and East Louisiana (January-February 1864)

McNair's-D. H. Reynolds' Brigade, Department of the Gulf (February-April 1864)

D. H. Reynolds' Brigade, District of the Gulf, Department of Alabama, Mississippi and East Louisiana (April-May 1864)

D. H. Reynolds' Brigade, Cantey's-Walthall's Division, Army of Mississippi (May-July 1864)

D. H. Reynolds' Brigade, Walthall's Division, 3rd Corps, Army of Tennessee (July 1864-April 1865)

**Battles:** Pea Ridge (March 7-8, 1862)
Corinth Campaign (April-June 1862)
Richmond, Kentucky (August 29-30, 1862)
Perryville (October 8, 1962)
Murfreesboro (December 31, 1862-January 3, 1863)
Jackson Siege (July 1863)
Chickamauga (September 19-20, 1863)
Chattanooga Siege (September-November 1863)
Atlanta Campaign (May-September 1864)
Dug Gap (May 8, 1864)
Resaca (May 14-15, 1864)
New Hope Church (May 25-June 4, 1864)
Kennesaw Mountain (June 27, 1864)
Moore's Hill (July 19, 1864)
Peach Tree Creek (July 20, 1864)
Atlanta (July 22, 1864)
Ezra Church (July 28, 1864)
Atlanta Siege (July-September 1864)
Lovejoy's Station (August 20, 1864)
Jonesboro (August 31-September 1, 1864)
Lovejoy's Station (September 2-5, 1864)
Moon's Station (October 3, 1864)
Franklin (November 30, 1864)
Nashville (December 15-16, 1864)
Sugar Creek (December 26, 1864)
Carolinas Campaign (February-April 1865)
Averasboro (March 16, 1865)
Bentonville (March 19-21, 1865)

**Further Reading:** Worley, Ted R., ed., *They Never Came Back: The Story of Co. F., Fourth Arkansas Infantry C.S.A.: The War Memoirs of Captain John W.*

*Lavender, C.S.A.* Gammage, Washington Lafayette, *The Camp, The Bivouac, and the Battlefield, Being a History of the Fourth Arkansas Regiment, from Its First Organization Down to the Present Date.*

## 104. ARKANSAS 4TH INFANTRY REGIMENT STATE TROOPS

**Organization:** Organized in June 1861. Mustered out in September 1861.
**First Commander:** James David Walker (Colonel)
**Assignment:** Pearce's Arkansas State Troops Brigade (June-September 1861)
**Battle:** Wilson's Creek (August 10, 1861)

## 105. ARKANSAS 4TH TRANS-MISSISSIPI INFANTRY REGIMENT

*See:* ARKANSAS 32ND INFANTRY REGIMENT

## 106. ARKANSAS 5TH INFANTRY REGIMENT

**Organization:** Organized for one year's state service at Gainesville on June 28, 1861. Transferred to Confederate service on July 27, 1861. Reorganized for two years at Tupelo, Mississippi, on May 12, 1862. Field consolidation with the 13th Infantry Regiment from August 1863 to April 9, 1865. Reenlisted for the war in January 1864. Additional field consolidation with the 1st, 2nd, 15th and 24th Infantry Regiments and the 3rd Confederate Infantry Regiment from December 1864 to April 9, 1865. 15th and 14th Infantry Regiments and the 3rd Confederate Infantry Regiment detached from this field consolidation in early 1865. Consolidated with the 1st, 2nd, 6th, 7th, 8th, 13th, 15th, 19th (Dawson's) and 24th Infantry Regiments and the 3rd Confederate Infantry Regiment Consolidated at Smithfield, North Carolina, on April 9, 1865.
**First Commander:** David C. Cross (Colonel)
**Field Officers:** T. W. Ellsberry (Major)
Lucius Featherston (Colonel)
Peter V. Green (Major, Lieutenant Colonel, Colonel)
E. A. Howell (Lieutenant Colonel)
John E. Murray (Lieutenant Colonel, Colonel)
Riddick Pope (Major)
Benjamin F. Sweeney (Lieutenant Colonel)
**Assignments:** Upper District of Arkansas (June-October 1861)
Cleburne's Brigade, Hardee's Division, Central Army of Kentucky, Department #2 (October 1861)
Wood's Brigade, Hardee's Division, Central Army of Kentucky, Department #2 (January-February 1862)
Hindman's Brigade, Hardee's Division, Central Army of Kentucky, Department #2 (February-March 1862)

Hindman's Brigade, 3rd Corps, Army of the Mississippi, Department #2 (March-July 1862)

Hindman's-Liddell's Brigade, Buckner's Division, Army of the Mississippi, Department #2 (July-August 1862)

Liddell's Brigade, Buckner's Division, Left Wing, Army of the Mississippi, Department #2 (August-November 1862)

Liddell's Brigade, Buckner's-Cleburne's Division, 2nd Corps, Army of Tennessee (November 1862-September 1863)

Liddell's Brigade, Liddell's Division, Reserve Corps, Army of Tennessee (September 1863)

Liddell's Brigade, Cleburne's Division, 2nd Corps, Army of Tennessee (October-November 1863)

Liddell's-Govan's Brigade, Cleburn's-Brown's Division, 1st Corps, Army of Tennessee (November 1863-April 1865)

**Battles:**   Corinth Campaign (April-June 1862)
Perryville (October 8, 1962)
Murfreesboro (December 31, 1862-January 3, 1863)
Tullahoma Campaign (June 1863)
Liberty Gap (June 24-26, 1863)
Chickamauga (September 19-20, 1863)
Chattanooga Siege (September-November 1863)
Chattanooga (November 23-25, 1863)
Ringgold Gap (November 27, 1863)
Atlanta Campaign (May-September 1864)
Dalton (May 5-11, 1864)
Resaca (May 14-15, 1864)
New Hope Church (May 25-June 4, 1864)
Kennesaw Mountain (June 27, 1864)
Peach Tree Creek (July 20, 1864)
Atlanta (July 22, 1864)
Atlanta Siege (July-September 1864)
Jonesboro (August 31-September 1, 1864)
Franklin (November 30, 1864)
Nashville (December 15-16, 1864)
Carolinas Campaign (February-April 1865)
Bentonville (March 19-21, 1865)

## 107.  ARKANSAS 5TH INFANTRY REGIMENT MILITIA

**Organization:**  Companies E and I mustered in on February 21, 1862. Mustered out on March 17, 1862.

## 108.  ARKANSAS 5TH INFANTRY REGIMENT STATE TROOPS

*Organization:*  Organized in June 1861. Mustered out in September 1861.
*First Commander:*  Thomas P. Dockery (Colonel)
*Field Officer:*  Joseph Neal (Lieutenant Colonel)
*Assignment:*  Pearce's Arkansas State Troops Brigade (June-September 1861)
*Battle:*  Wilson's Creek (August 10, 1861)

## 109.  ARKANSAS 5TH TRANS-MISSISSIPPI INFANTRY REGIMENT

*See:*  ARKANSAS 30TH INFANTRY REGIMENT

## 110.  ARKANSAS 6TH INFANTRY REGIMENT

*Organization:*  Organized at Little Rock in June 1861. Mustered into state service on June 7, 1861. Mustered into Confederate service on July 26, 1861. Reorganized on June 5, 1862. Portion of 12th Infantry Regiment not captured at Island #10 served as 2nd Companies D and F from June 16, 1862, to September 1862, when regiment was reconstituted. Field consolidated with the 7th Infantry Regiment from December 22, 1862, to April 9, 1865. Consolidated with 1st, 2nd, 5th, 7th, 8th, 13th, 15th, 19th (Dawson's) and 24th Infantry Regiments and the 3rd Confederate Infantry Regiment Consolidated at Smithfield, North Carolina, on April 9, 1865.
*First Commander:*  Richard Lyon (Colonel)
*Field Officers:*  F. J. Cameron (Major)
William F. Douglas (Major)
J. B. Gordon (Major)
Alexander T. Hawthorn, (Lieutenant Colonel, Colonel)
Dawson L. Kilgore (Major)
Gordon N. Peay (Lieutenant Colonel)
Samuel G. Smith (Major, Colonel)
*Assignments:*  Upper District of Arkansas (June-October 1861)
Hindman's Brigade, Hardee's Division, Central Army of Kentucky, Department #2 (October 1861-March 1862)
Hindman's Brigade, 3rd Corps, Army of the Mississippi, Department #2 (March-July 1862)
Hindman's-Liddell's Brigade, Buckner's Division, Army of the Mississippi, Department #2 (July-August 1862)
Liddell's Brigade, Buckner's Division, Left Wing, Army of the Mississippi, Department #2 (August-November 1862)
Liddell's Brigade, Buckner's-Cleburnes Division, 2nd Corps, Army of Tennessee (November 1862-September 1863)
Liddell's Brigade, Liddell's Division, Reserve Corps, Army of Tennessee (September 1863)

Liddell's Brigade, Cleburne's Division, 2nd Corps, Army of Tennessee (October-November 1863)

Liddell's-Govan's Brigade, Cleburne's Brown's Division, 1st Corps, Army of Tennessee (November 1863-April 1865)

**Battles:**  Woodsonville, Kentucky (December 17, 1861)

Shiloh (April 6-7, 1862)

Corinth Campaign (April 1862-June 1862)

Perryville (October 8, 1862)

Murfreesboro (December 31, 1862-January 3, 1983)

Tullahoma Campaign (June 1863)

Liberty Gap (June 24-26, 1863)

Chickamauga (September 19-20, 1863)

Chattanooga Siege (September-November 1863)

Chattanooga (November 23-25, 1863)

Ringgold Gap (November 27, 1863)

Atlanta Campaign (May-September 1864)

Dalton (May 5-11, 1864)

Resaca (May 14-15, 1864)

New Hope Church (May 25-June 4, 1864)

Kennesaw Mountain (June 27, 1864)

Peach Tree Creek (July 20, 1864)

Atlanta (July 22, 1864)

Atlanta Siege (July-September 1864)

Jonesboro (August 31-September 1, 1864)

Franklin (November 30, 1864)

Nashville (December 15-16, 1864)

Carolinas Campaign (February-April 1865)

Bentonville (March 19-21, 1865)

**Further Reading:**  Collier, Calvin L., *First In—Last Out: The Capitol Guards, Arkansas Brigade.*

## 111. ARKANSAS 6TH TRANS-MISSISSIPPI INFANTRY REGIMENT

*See:*  ARKANSAS JOHNSON'S-HAWTHORN'S-COCKE'S INFANTRY REGIMENT

## 112. ARKANSAS 7TH INFANTRY BATTALION

**Also Known As:**  Arkansas 7th Cavalry Battalion (So listed in *Confederate Cavalry West of the Mississippi River*)

**Organization:**  Organized with six companies ca. October 1861. Consolidated into three companies and assigned to the 8th Infantry Regiment on May 7, 1862.

**First Commander:**  Franklin W. Desha (Major, Lieutenant Colonel)

*Field Officer:*  Jesse N. Cypert (Major)

*Assignments:*  Upper District of Arkansas, Department #2 (November 1861-January 1862)

Mouton's Brigade, 1st Corps, 2nd Grand Division, Army of the Mississippi, Department #2 (March 1862)

Jackson's Brigade, Withers' Division, 2nd Corps, Army of the Mississippi, Department #2 (March-May 1862)

## 113.  ARKANSAS 7TH INFANTRY REGIMENT

*Organization:*  Organized at Smithfield, Lawrence County, on June 16, 1861. Mustered into Confederate service on July 26, 1861. Reorganized at Corinth, Mississippi, on May 14, 1862. Field consolidated with the 6th Infantry Regiment from December 22, 1862, to April 9, 1865. Consolidated with 1st, 2nd, 5th, 6th, 8th, 15th, 19th (Dawson's) and 24th Infantry Regiments and the 3rd Confederate Infantry Regiment and designated as the 1st Infantry Regiment Consolidated at Smithfield, North Carolina, on April 9, 1865.

*First Commander:*  Robert G. Shaver (Colonel)

*Field Officers:*  William R. Cain (Lieutenant Colonel)

John M. Dean (Major, Lieutenant Colonel)

D. A. Gillespie (Colonel)

J. A. Hill (Major)

James T. Martin (Major)

J. C. McCauley (Major)

J. Rutherford (Lieutenant Colonel)

Peter Snyder (Lieutenant Colonel, Colonel)

*Assignments:*  Upper District of Arkansas (June-October 1861)

Shaver's-Wood's Brigade, Hardee's Division, Central Army of Kentucky, Department #2 (October 1861-February 1862)

Hindman's Brigade, Hardee's Division, Central Army of Kentucky, Department #2 (February-March 1862)

Hindman's Brigade, 3rd Corps, Army of the Mississippi, Department #2 (March-July 1862)

Hindman's-Liddell's Brigade, Buckner's Division, Army of the Mississippi, Department #2 (July-August 1862)

Liddell's Brigade, Buckner's Division, Left Wing, Army of the Mississippi, Department #2 (August-November 1862)

Liddell's Brigade, Buckner's-Cleburne's Division, 2nd Corps, Army of Tennessee, (November 1862-September 1863)

Liddell's Brigade, Liddell's Division, Reserve Corps, Army of Tennessee (September 1863)

Liddell's Brigade, Cleburne's Division, 2nd Corps, Army of Tennessee (October-November 1863)
Liddell's-Govan's Brigade, Cleburne's-Brown's Division, 1st Corps, Army of Tennessee (November 1863-April 1865)
**Battles:** Shiloh (April 6-7, 1862)
Corinth Campaign (April-June 1862)
Perryville (October 8, 1862)
Murfreesboro (December 31, 1862-January 3, 1983)
Tullahoma Campaign (June 1863)
Liberty Gap (June 24-26, 1863)
Chickamauga (September 19-20, 1863)
Chattanooga Siege (September-November 1863)
Chattanooga (November 23-25, 1863)
Ringgold Gap (November 27, 1863)
Atlanta Campaign (May-September 1864)
Dalton (May 5-11, 1864)
Resaca (May 14-15, 1864)
New Hope Church (May 25-June 4, 1864)
Kennesaw Mountain (June 27, 1864)
Peach Tree Creek (July 20, 1864)
Atlanta (July 22, 1864)
Atlanta Siege (July-September 1864)
Jonesboro (August 31-September 1, 1864)
Franklin (November 30, 1864)
Nashville (December 15-16, 1864)
Carolinas Campaign (February-April 1865)
Bentonville (March 19-21, 1865)

## 114. ARKANSAS 7TH INFANTRY REGIMENT MILITIA
*Organization:* Mustered in with five companies on February 22, 1862.
*First Commander:* A. L. Berry (Colonel)
*Field Officers:* W. B. Crook (Major)
T. N. Lane (Lieutenant Colonel)

## 115. ARKANSAS 8TH INFANTRY BATTALION
*Also Known As:* Arkansas 1st (Jones') Infantry Battalion
*Organization:* Organized with seven companies in early 1862. Surrendered at Port Hudson, Louisiana, on July 8, 1863.
*First Commander:* Bart. Jones (Lieutenant Colonel)
*Field Officers:* John Miller (Major)
M. R. Wilson (Major)

*Assignments:* Rust's-Dockery's-Cabell's Brigade, Jones'-Maury's Division, Army of the West, Department #2 (April-September 1862)

Cabell's Brigade, Maury's Division, Price's Corps, Army of West Tennessee, Department of Mississippi and East Louisiana (October 1862)

Cabell's Brigade, Bowen's Division, Price's Corps, Army of North Mississippi, Department of Mississippi and East Louisiana (October-December 1862)

Cravens' Brigade, Bowen's Division, Price's Corps, Army of North Mississippi, Department of Mississippi and East Louisiana (October-December 1862)

Beall's Brigade, 3rd Military District, Department of Mississippi and East Louisiana (January-July 1863)

*Battles:* Corinth Campaign (April-June 1862)

Corinth (October 3-4, 1862)

Port Hudson Siege (May-July 1863)

## 116. ARKANSAS 8TH INFANTRY REGIMENT

*Organization:* Organized at Jacksonport on July 13, 1861. Mustered into Confederate service for 12 months on September 10, 1861. Reduced to five companies and reorganized by the assignment of the 7th and 9th Infantry Battalions on May 7, 1862. Field consolidation with the 19th (Dawson's) Infantry Regiment from November 15, 1863, to April 9, 1865. Consolidated with 1st, 2nd, 5th, 6th, 7th, 13th, 15th, 19th (Dawson's) and 24th Infantry Regiments and the 3rd Confederate Infantry Regiment and designated as the 1st Infantry Regiment Consolidated at Smithfield, North Carolina, on April 9, 1865.

*First Commander:* William K. Patterson (Colonel)

*Field Officers:* George F. Baucum (Major, Lieutenant Colonel, Colonel)

H. M. Couch (Lieutenant Colonel)

John H. Kelly (Colonel)

John A. Price (Major)

Anderson Watkins (Major, Lieutenant Colonel)

James H. Wilson (Lieutenant Colonel)

W. P. Witt (Major)

*Assignments:* Shaver's-Wood's Brigade, Hardee's Division, Central Army of Kentucky, Department #2 (October 1861-February 1862)

Wood's Brigade, Pillow's Division, Central Army of Kentucky, Department #2 (February-March 1862)

Wood's Brigade, 3rd Corps, Army of the Mississippi, Department #2 (March-May 1862)

Liddell's Brigade, 3rd Corps, Army of the Mississippi, Department #2 (June-July 1862)

Liddell's Brigade, Buckner's Division, Army of the Mississippi, Department #2 (July-August 1862)

Liddell's Brigade, Buckner's Division, Left Wing, Army of the Mississippi, Department #2 (August-November 1862)

Liddell's Brigade, Buckner's-Cleburne's Division, 2nd Corps, Army of Tennessee, (November 1862-September 1863)

Liddell's Brigade, Liddell's Division, Reserve Corps, Army of Tennessee (September 1863)

Liddell's Brigade, Cleburne's Division, 2nd Corps, Army of Tennessee (October-November 1863)

Liddell's-Govan's Brigade, Cleburne's-Brown's Division, 1st Corps, Army of Tennessee (November 1863-April 1865)

**Battles:**  Shiloh (April 6-7, 1862)

Corinth Campaign (April 1862-June 1862)

Perryville (October 8, 1862)

Murfreesboro (December 31, 1862-January 3, 1983)

Tullahoma Campaign (June 1863)

Liberty Gap (not engaged) (June 24-26, 1863)

Chickamauga (September 19-20, 1863)

Chattanooga Siege (September-November 1863)

Chattanooga (November 23-25, 1863)

Ringgold Gap (November 27, 1863)

Atlanta Campaign (May-September 1864)

Dalton (May 5-11, 1864)

Resaca (May 14-15, 1864)

New Hope Church (May 25-June 4, 1864)

Kennesaw Mountain (June 27, 1864)

Pickett's Mill (May 27, 1864)

Peach Tree Creek (July 20, 1864)

Atlanta (July 22, 1864)

Atlanta Siege (July-September 1864)

Jonesboro (August 31-September 1, 1864)

Franklin (November 30, 1864)

Nashville (December 15-16, 1864)

Carolinas Campaign (February-April 1865)

Bentonville (March 19-21, 1865)

## 117.  ARKANSAS 9TH INFANTRY BATTALION

**Organization:** Organized by the assignment of four companies of the 14th (McCarver's) Infantry Regiment in January 1862. Consolidated into two companies and became 2nd Companies F and G, 8th Infantry Regiment, on May 7, 1862.

**First Commander:**  John H. Kelly (Major)

*Assignments:* Wood's Brigade, Hardee's Divsion, Central Army of Kentucky, Department #2 (January-February 1862)
Wood's Brigade, Pillow's Division, Central Army of Kentucky, Department #2 (February-March 1862)
Wood's Brigade, 3rd Corps, Army of the Mississippi, Department #2 (March-May 1862)
*Battle:* Shiloh (April 6-7, 1862)

## 118. ARKANSAS 9TH INFANTRY REGIMENT

*Organization:* Organized at Pine Bluff on July 20, 1861. Mustered into state service between July 25 and 27, 1861. Consolidated with the 1st and 2nd Mounted Rifles Regiments, 4th Infantry Battalion and the 4th and 25th Infantry Regiments and designated as the 1st Mounted Rifles Regiment Consolidated at Smithfield, North Carolina, on April 9, 1865.

*First Commander:* John M. Bradley (Colonel)

*Field Officers:* John C. Bratton (Major)
Isaac L. Dunlop (Colonel)
W. Y. McCammon (Lieutenant Colonel)
Reuben W. Millsaps (Lieutenant Colonel)
Jefferson W. Rogers (Lieutenant Colonel)
R. M. Wallace (Major)
W. J. Wallace (Sr. Major)

*Assignments:* Travis' Brigade, Pillow's Division, 1st Geographical Division, Department #2 (October-November 1861)
1st Brigade, Bowen's Division, 1st Geographical Division, Department #2 (November-December 1861)
Bowen's Brigade, Central Army of Kentucky, Department #2 (December 1861-January 1862)
Bowen's Brigade, Pillow's Division, Central Army of Kentucky, Department #2 (February-March 1862)
Bowen's Brigade, Reserve Corps, Army of the Mississippi, Department #2 (March-April 1862)
Helm's Brigade, Reserve Corps, Army of the Mississippi, Department #2 (May-June 1862)
Department of Southern Mississippi and East Louisiana (June-July, 1862)
District of the Mississippi, Department #2 (July-August 1862)
Rust's Brigade, Lovell's Division, Department of Mississippi and East Louisiana (October 1862)
Rust's Brigade, Lovell's Division, Department of Mississippi and East Louisiana (October-December 1862)

Rust's Division, 1st Corps, Army of North Mississippi, Department of Mississippi and East Louisiana (December 1862-January 1863)

Rust's Brigade, Loring's Division, Army of North Mississippi, Department of Mississippi and East Louisiana(January-February 1863)

Rust's Brigade, 3rd Military District, Department of Mississippi and East Louisiana (March-April 1863)

Buford's Brigade, Loring's Division, Department of Mississippi and East Louisiana (April-May 1863)

Buford's Brigade, Loring's Division Department of the West (May-July 1863)

Buford's Brigade, Loring's Division, Department of Mississippi and East Louisiana (July 1863-January 1864)

Bufford's-Scott's Brigade, Loring's Division, Department of Alabama, Mississippi and East Louisiana (January-May 1864)

D. H. Reynolds' Brigade, Cantey's-Walthall's Division, Army of Mississippi (May-July 1864)

D. H. Reynolds' Brigade, Walthall's Division, 3rd Corps, Army of Tennessee (July 1864-April 1865)

**Battles:**   Corinth Campaign (April 1862-June 1862)
Vicksburg Bombardments (May 18-July 27, 1862)
Corinth (October 3-4, 1862)
Coffeeville (December 15, 1862)
Vicksburg Campaign (May-July 1863)
Champion Hill (May 16, 1863)
Jackson Siege (July 1863)
Meridian Campaign (February-March 1864)
Atlanta Campaign (May-September 1864)
Resaca (May 14-15, 1864)
New Hope Church (May 25-June 4, 1864)
Kennesaw Mountain (June 27, 1864)
Dug Gap (May 8, 1864)
Peach Tree Creek (July 20, 1864)
Atlanta (July 22, 1864)
Ezra Church (July 28, 1864)
Atlanta Siege (July-September 1864)
Lovejoy's Station (September 2-5, 1864)
Jonesboro (August 31-September 1, 1864)
Franklin (November 30, 1864)
Nashville (December 15-16, 1864)
Sugar Creek (December 26, 1864)
Carolinas Campaign (February-April 1865)
Bentonville (March 19-21, 1865)

## 119. ARKANSAS 9TH (MCCARVER'S) INFANTRY REGIMENT

*See:* ARKANSAS 14TH (MCCARVER'S) INFANTRY REGIMENT

## 120. ARKANSAS 10TH INFANTRY BATTALION

*Organization:* This organization with an unknown number of companies is not listed at the National Archives or in the *Official Records.*

*First Commander:* R. Scott (Lieutenant Colonel)

## 121. ARKANSAS 10TH INFANTRY REGIMENT

*Organization:* Organized at Springfield, Conway County, in July 1861. Reduced to eight companies ca. April 1862. Reorganized May 8, 1862. Surrendered at Port Hudson, Louisiana, on July 8, 1863. Paroled later in month. Declared exchanged at some time in 1864. Mounted and consolidated with the remnants of other regiments and designated as the 10th Cavalry Regiment in the summer of 1864.

*First Commander:* Thomas D. Merrick (Colonel)

*Field Officers:* C. M. Cargile (Major)

S. S. Ford (Lieutenant Colonel)

Obed. Patty (Major)

Luther R. Venable (Lieutenant Colonel)

Allan R. Witt (Colonel)

*Assignments:* Bowen's Brigade, 1st Geographical Division, Department #2 (October 1861)

Bonham's Brigade, Bowen's Division, 1st Geographical Division, Department #2 (October-December 1861)

Bowen's Brigade, Central Army of Kentucky, Department #2 (January-February 1862)

Bowen's Brigade, Pillow's Division, Central Army of Kentucky, Department #2 (February-March 1862)

Bowen's Brigade, Reserve Corps, Army of the Mississippi, Department #2 (March-April 1862)

Helm's Brigade, Reserve Corps, Army of the Mississippi, Department #2 (May-June 1862)

3rd Military District, Department of the Mississippi and East Louisiana (October 1862)

Buford's Brigade, 3rd Military District, Department of the Mississippi and East Louisiana (March-April 1863)

Maxey's Brigade, 3rd Military District, Department of the Mississippi and East Louisiana (April 1863)

Beall's Brigade, 3rd Military District, Department of the Mississippi and East Louisiana (May-July 1863)

**Battles:** Shiloh (April 6-7, 1862)
Corinth Campaign (April-June 1862)
Vicksburg Bombardments (May 18-July 27, 1862)
Port Hudson Siege (May-July 1863)

## 122. ARKANSAS 10TH INFANTRY REGIMENT MILITIA

**Organization:** Mustered in on February 22, 1862. Mustered out on March 19, 1862.
**First Commander:** J. W. May (Colonel)
**Field Officers:** H. G. Butts (Major)
A. D. King (Lieutenant Colonel)

## 123. ARKANSAS 11TH INFANTRY BATTALION

**Organization:** Organized with nine companies in early 1862. Reorganized on May 8, 1862. Increased to a regiment by the assignment of one company from the 8th Infantry Battalion and designated as the 25th Infantry Regiment (AKA: 30th Infantry Regiment in 1862) on June 18, 1862.
**First Commander:** B. G. Johnson (Lieutenant Colonel)
**Field Officer:** Charles J. Turnbull (Lieutenant Colonel)
**Assignment:** Churchill's Brigade, McCown's Division, Army of the West, Department #2 (April-June 1862)
**Battle:** Corinth Campaign (April-June 1862)

## 124. ARKANSAS 11TH INFANTRY REGIMENT

**Organization:** Organized for one year in Saline County in July 1861. Surrendered at Island #10 on April 7, 1862. Exchanged at Vicksburg, Warren County, Mississippi, on September 16, 1862. Reorganized at Jackson, Mississippi, in October 1862. Field consolidation with the 15th Infantry Regiment in early 1863. Consolidated with the 17th (Rector's-Griffith's) Infantry Regiment and designated as the 11th and 17th Infantry Regiment Consolidated in January 1863.
**First Commander:** Jabez M. Smith (Colonel)
**Field Officers:** John L. Logan (Colonel)
Mark S. Miller (Lieutenant Colonel)
James T. Poe (Major)
McDuff Vance (Lieutenant Colonel)
**Assignments:** Fort Pillow, 1st Geographical Division, Department #2 (November 1861-January 1862)
New Madrid, 1st Geographical Division, Department #2 (January-February 1862)

Gantt's Brigade, McCown's Command, 1st Geographical Division, Department #2 (February-April 1862)
3rd Military District, Department of the Mississippi and East Louisiana (October 1862)
Beall's Brigade, 3rd Military District, Department of the Mississippi and East Louisiana (January 1863)
**Battle:** Island #10 (April 6-7, 1862)
**Further Reading:** Poe, J. C., ed., *The Raving Foe: The Civil War Diary of Major James T. Poe, C.S.A., and the 11th Arkansas Volunteers and a Complete List of Prisoners.*

## 125. ARKANSAS 11TH AND 17TH (MOUNTED) INFANTRY REGIMENT CONSOLIDATED

**Organization:** Organized by the consolidation of the 11th and 17th (Rector's-Griffith's) Infantry Regiments in January 1863. Mounted in May 1863. Unmounted detachment surrendered at Port Hudson, Louisiana, on July 8, 1863. Paroled later in month. Furloughed in September 1863. Surrendered by General E. Kirby Smith, commanding the Trans-Mississippi Department, on May 26, 1856.
**First Commander:** John Griffith (Colonel)
**Field Officers:** Benjamin P. Jett (Major)
John L. Logan (Colonel)
McDuff Vance (Lieutenant Colonel)
**Assignments:** Beall's Brigade, 3rd Military District, Department of Mississippi and East Louisiana (January-July 1863)
Logan's Cavalry Brigade, 3rd Military District, Department of Mississippi and East Louisiana (June-July 1863)
Logan's Cavalry Brigade, Department of Mississippi and East Louisiana (July-September 1863)
W. Adams' Brigade, Jackson's Division, Lee's Cavalry Corps, Department of Mississippi and East Louisiana (November 1863-January 1864)
W. Adams' Brigade, Jackson's Division, Lee's Cavalry Corps, Department of Alabama, Mississippi and East Louisiana (January-May 1864)
Mabry's Brigade, W. Adams' Cavalry Division, Department of Alabama, Mississippi and East Louisiana (May-August 1864)
Mabry's Brigade, District North of Homochitto (W. Adams), Department of Alabama, Mississippi and East Louisiana (August 1864)
Cavalry, Arkansas (Churchill's) Division, District of Arkansas, Trans-Mississippi Department (August-September 1864)
Unattached, 1st (Wharton's) Texas Cavalry Division, 2nd Corps, Trans-Mississippi Department (September 1864-May 1865)

*Battles:* Port Hudson Siege (May-July 1863)
near Natchez (November 7, 1863)
Meridian Campaign (February-March 1864)
Concord Church, Mississippi (December 1, 1864)

### 126. ARKANSAS 12TH INFANTRY BATTALION SHARPSHOOTERS

*Organization:* Organized with four companies, each one composed of men selected from the 18th, 19th (Dockery's), 20th and 21st (Craven's) Infantry Regiments in June 1862. Regiment surrendered at Vicksburg, Warren County, Mississippi, on July 4, 1863. Paroled there later in month. Apparently never reorganized. There is one reference to the battalion on April 20, 1864, as being in Fagan's Cavalry Division, District of Arkansas, Trans-Mississippi Department. Was probably a fragment of the command serving mounted in its home state.

*First Commander:* William F. Rapley (Major)

*Field Officer:* C. L. Jackson (Major) (temporary assignment)

*Assignments:* Dockery's-Cabell's Brigade, Maury's Division, Army of the West Department #2 (June-September 1862)

Cabell's Brigade, Maury's Division, Price's Corps, Army of West Tennessee, Department #2 (September-October 1862)

Cabell's Brigade, Price's Corps, Army of West Tennessee, Department of Mississippi and East Louisiana (October 1862)

Hébert's Brigade, Bowen's Division, Price's Corps, Army of West Tennessee, Department of Mississippi and East Louisiana (October 1862)

Craven's Brigade, Bowen's Division, Price's Corps, Army of West Tennessee, Department of Mississippi and East Louisiana (October-December 1862)

Craven's-Green's Brigade, Bowen's Division, 2nd Corps, Army of North Mississippi, Department of Mississippi and East Louisiana (December 1862-January 1863)

Green's Brigade, Price's-Forney's Division, Army of North Mississippi, Department of Mississippi and East Louisiana (January-February 1863)

Green's Brigade, Forney's-Bowen's Division, 2nd Military District, Department of Mississippi and East Louisiana (March-April 1863)

Green's Brigade, Bowen's Division, Department of Mississippi and East Louisiana (April-July 1863)

*Battles:* Corinth (October 3-4, 1862)
Steele's Bayou Expedition (March 14-27, 1863)
Rolling Fork (March 20, 1863)
Grand Gulf (April 29, 1863)
Vicksburg Campaign (May-July 1863)

Port Gibson (May 1, 1863)
Champion Hill (May 16, 1863)
Big Black River Bridge (May 17, 1863)
Vicksburg Siege (May-July 1863)
Camden Expedition (March-May 1864)
Marks' Mill (April 25, 1864)

## 127. ARKANSAS 12TH INFANTRY REGIMENT

*Organization:* Organized on July 27, 1861, Surrendered at Island #10 on April 7, 1862. Men of the regiment who were not captured served in the 3rd and 6th Infantry Regiments until the regiment was reorganized. Exchanged in late 1862. Reorganized at Jackson, Mississippi, on October 2, 1862. Surrendered at Port Hudson, Louisiana, on July 8, 1863. Paroled later in month. Consolidated with other units and designated as the 2nd Infantry Regiment Consolidated, Trans-Mississippi Department, on January 11, 1864.

*First Commander:* Edward W. Gantt (Colonel)
*Field Officers:* W. D. S. Cook (Lieutenant Colonel)
Edward C. Jordan (Lieutenant Colonel)
Thomas J. Reid, Jr. (Major, Colonel)
John S. Walker (Major)

*Assignments:* New Madrid, 1st Geographical Division, Department #2 (January-February 1862)
Gantt's Brigade, McCown's Command, 1st Geographical Division, Department #2 (February-April 1862)
Beall's Brigade, 3rd Military District, Department of Mississippi and East Louisiana (March-July 1863)

*Battles:* Island #10 (April 6-7, 1862)
Port Hudson Siege (May-July 1863)

## 128. ARKANSAS 13TH INFANTRY REGIMENT

*Organization:* Organized on July 29, 1861. Mustered into Confederate service for 12 months on July 23, 1861. Company K, 7th Kentucky Infantry Regiment, assigned as 2nd Company E on April 13, 1862. Reorganized for two years or the war on April 29, 1862. Field consolidation with the 15th Infantry Regiment during much of 1863. Field consolidation with the 5th Infantry Regiment from August 1863 to April 9, 1865. Additional field consolidation with the 1st, 2nd, 15th and 24th Infantry Regiments and the 3rd Confederate Infantry Regiment in early 1865. Consolidated with 1st, 2nd, 5th, 6th, 7th, 8th, 15th, 19th (Dawson's) and 24th Infantry Regiments and designated as the 1st Infantry Regiment Consolidated at Smithfield, North Carolina, on April 9, 1865.

*First Commander:* James C. Tappan (Colonel)

*Field Officers:* A. R. Brown (Lieutenant Colonel)
Robert A. Duncan (Major, Lieutenant Colonel)
A. D. Grayson (Lieutenant Colonel)
E. A. Howell (Major)
George B. Hunt (Major)
James A. McNeely (Major, Colonel)
J. M. Pollard (Lieutenant Colonel)

*Assignments:* Travis' Brigade, Pillow's Division 1st Geographical Division, Department #2 (October 1861-January 1862)
2nd Division, 1st Geographical Division, Department #2 (January-March 1862)
Tappan's Brigade, 1st Grand Division, Army of the Mississippi, Department #2 (March-July 1862)
Stewart's Brigade, Clark's Division, 1st Corps, Army of the Mississippi, Department #2 (March-July 1862)
Cleburne's Brigade, Buckner's Division, Army of the Mississippi, Department #2 (July-August 1862)
Cleburne's-Polk's Brigade, Buckner's-Cleburne's Division, Left Wing, Army of the Mississippi, Department #2 (August-November 1862)
Polk's Brigade, Cleburne's Division, 2nd Corps, Army of Tennessee (November 1862-January 1863)
Liddell's Brigade, Cleburn's Division, 2nd Corps, Army of Tennessee (July-September 1863)
Liddell's Brigade, Liddell's Division, Reserve Corps, Army of Tennessee (September 1863)
Liddell's Brigade, Cleburne's Division, 2nd Corps, Army of Tennessee (September-November 1863)
Liddell's-Govan's Brigade, Cleburne's Division, 1st Corps, Army of Tennessee (November 1863-April 1865)

*Battles:* Belmont (November 7, 1861)
Shiloh (April 6-7, 1862)
Corinth Campaign (April-June 1862)
Richmond, Kentucky (August 29-30, 1862)
Perryville (October 8, 1862)
Murfreesboro (December 31, 1862-January 3, 1983)
Tullahoma Campaign (June 1863)
Liberty Gap (June 24-26, 1863)
Chickamauga (September 19-20, 1863)
Chattanooga Siege (September-November 1863)
Chattanooga (November 23-25, 1863)
Ringgold Gap (November 27, 1863)

Atlanta Campaign (May-September 1864)
Dalton (May 5-11, 1864)
Resaca (May 14-15, 1864)
New Hope Church (May 25-June 4, 1864)
Kennesaw Mountain (June 27, 1864)
Peach Tree Creek (July 20, 1864)
Atlanta (July 22, 1864)
Atlanta Siege (July-September 1864)
Jonesboro (August 31-September 1, 1864)
Franklin (November 30, 1864)
Nashville (December 15-16, 1864)
Carolinas Campaign (February-April 1865)
Bentonville (March 19-21, 1865)

## 129.  ARKANSAS 13TH INFANTRY REGIMENT MILITIA

*Organization:*  Mustered in with seven identified companies on February 24, 1862. Mustered out on March 9, 1862.

## 130.  ARKANSAS 14TH (MCCARVER'S) INFANTRY REGIMENT

*Also Known As:*  Arkansas 9th (McCarver's) Infantry Regiment
Arkansas 18th Infantry Battalion (after the four companies were transferred to the 9th Infantry Battalion)
*Organization:*  Organized and mustered into Confederate service for 12 months at Pocahontas on September 23, 1861. Companies A, B, E and H detached from the regiment and designated as the 9th Infantry Battalion in January 1862. Balance of the regiment often referred to as the 18th Infantry Battalion. Six remaining companies consolidated into four on May 14, 1862. Consolidated with the 17th (Lemoyne's) Infantry Regiment and designated as the 21st Infantry Regiment on May 14, 1862.
*First Commander:*  John S. McCarver (Colonel)
*Field Officers:*  John H. Kelly (Major)
Samuel J. Mason (Lieutenant Colonel)
*Assignment:*  Rust's Brigade, Jones' Division, Army of the West, Department #2 (April-May 1862)
*Battle:*  Corinth Campaign (April-June 1862)

## 131.  ARKANSAS 14TH (MITCHELL'S-POWERS') INFANTRY REGIMENT

*Organization:*  Organized in the summer or fall of 1861. Reorganized on May 16, 1862. Field consolidation with the 18th and 23rd Infantry Regiment from February 1863 to July 1863. Surrendered at Port Hudson, Louisiana, on July 8,

1863. Paroled later in month. Consolidated with the 15th Northwest, 16th and 21st Infantry Regiments and designated as the 1st Infantry Regiment Consolidated, Trans-Mississippi Department, in January 1864.
**First Commander:**   William C. Mitchell (Colonel)
**Field Officers:**   John Allin (Major)
Eli Dodson (Lieutenant Colonel, Colonel)
Pleasant Fowler, (Lieutenant Colonel, Colonel)
H. E. Messick (Major)
J. H. Messick (Major)
Frank P. Powers (Colonel)
**Assignments:**   McCulloch's Division, Department #2 (October-December 1861)
Hébert's Brigade, McCulloch's Division, Department #2 (December 1861-January 1862)
Hébert's Brigade, McCulloch's Division, Trans-Mississippi District, Department #2 (January-March 1862)
Hébert's Brigade, Price's Division, Trans-Mississippi District, Department #2 (March-April 1862)
Hébert's Brigade, Price's-Little's Division, Army of the West, Department #2 (April-September 1862)
Hébert's Brigade, Little's-Hébert's Division, Price's Corps, Army of West Tennessee, Department of Mississippi and East Louisiana (September-October 1862)
Hébert's Brigade, Bowen's Division, Price's Corps, Army of West Tennessee, Department of Mississippi and East Louisiana (October 1862)
Craven's Brigade, Bowen's Division, Price's Corps, Army of West Tennessee, Department of Mississippi and East Louisiana (October-December 1862)
Craven's Brigade, Bowen's Division, 2nd Corps, Army of North Mississippi, Department of Mississippi and East Louisiana (December 1862)
Beale's Brigade, 3rd Military District, Department of Mississippi and East Louisiana (January-July 1863)
**Battles:**   Pea Ridge (March 7-8, 1862)
Corinth Campaign (April-June 1862)
Iuka (September 19, 1862)
Corinth (October 3-4, 1862)
Port Hudson Siege (May-July 1863)

## 132.   ARKANSAS 15TH INFANTRY REGIMENT

**Organization:** Organized by the change of designation of the 1st Infantry Regiment, State Troops, to the 1st (Cleburne's) Infantry Regiment on July 23, 1861. Designated as the 15th Infantry Regiment by the War Department on

December 31, 1861. Field consolidation with the 13th Infantry Regiment during part of 1863. Field consolidation with the 2nd Infantry Regiment from the summer of 1863 to early 1864. Additional field consolidation with the 24th Infantry Regiment from November 16, 1863, to early 1864. Field consolidation with the 1st Infantry Regiment from early 1864 to early 1865. Additional field consolidation with the 2nd, 5th, 13th and 24th Infantry Regiments and the 3rd Confederate Infantry Regiment in early 1865. New field consolidation with the 24th Infantry Regiment and the 3rd Confederate Infantry Regiment in early 1865. Consolidated with 1st, 2nd, 5th, 6th, 7th, 8th, 13th, 19th (Dawson's) and 24th Infantry Regiments and the 3rd Confederate Infantry Regiment and designated as the 1st Infantry Regiment Consolidated at Smithfield, North Carolina, on April 9, 1865.

*First Commander:*  Patrick E. Cleburne (Colonel)
*Field Officers:*  Samuel S. Black (Lieutenant Colonel)
Charles H. Carlton (Major)
James T. Harris (Major)
John E. Josey (Major, Lieutenant Colonel, Colonel)
Archibald K. Patton (Lieutenant Colonel)
Lucius E. Polk (Colonel)
*Assignments:*  Upper District of Arkansas (July-September 1861)
Cleburne's Brigade, Hardee's Division, Central Army of Kentucky, Department #2 (October 1861-March 1862)
Cleburne's Brigade, 3rd Corps, Army of the Mississippi, Department #2 (March-July 1862)
Cleburne's Brigade, Buckner's Division, Army of the Mississippi, Department #2 (July-August 1862)
Cleburne's Brigade, Buckner's Division, Left Wing, Army of the Mississippi, Department #2 (August-November 1862)
Cleburne's-Polk's Brigade, Buckner's-Cleburne's Division, 2nd Corps, Army of Tennessee (November 1862-January 1863)
Liddell's Brigade, Cleburne's Division, 2nd Corps, Army of Tennessee (July-September 1863)
Liddell's Brigade, Liddell's Division, 2nd Corps, Army of Tennessee (September 1863)
Liddell's Brigade, Cleburne's Division, 2nd Corps, Army of Tennessee (September-November 1863)
Liddell's Brigade, Cleburne's Division, 1st Corps, (November 1863-January 1864)
Polk's Brigade, Cleburne's Division, 1st Corps, Army of Tennessee (April-July 1864)
Govan's Brigade, Cleburne's Division, 1st Corps, Army of Tennessee (July 1864-April 1865)

**Battles:** Shiloh (April 6-7, 1862)
Perryville (October 8, 1862)
Murfreesboro (December 31, 1862-January 3, 1983)
Tullahoma Campaign (June 1863)
Liberty Gap (June 24-26, 1863)
Chickamauga (September 19-20, 1863)
Chattanooga Siege (September-November 1863)
Chattanooga (November 23-25, 1863)
Atlanta Campaign (May-September 1864)
Dalton (May 5-11, 1864)
Resaca (May 14-15, 1864)
New Hope Church (May 25-June 4, 1864)
Kennesaw Mountain (June 27, 1864)
Atlanta (July 22, 1864)
Atlanta Siege (July-September 1864)
Jonesboro (August 31-September 1, 1864)
Franklin (November 30, 1864)
Nashville (December 15-16, 1864)
Carolinas Campaign (February-April 1865)

### 133. ARKANSAS 15TH INFANTRY REGIMENT MILITIA

*Organization:* Mustered in on March 10, 1862. Mustered out on March 11, 1862. Became Williamson's Infantry Battalion ca. March 1862.
*First Commander:* John L. Williamson (Colonel)
*Field Officers:* E. M. Roach (Major)
George M. P. Williamson (Lieutenant Colonel)

### 134. ARKANSAS 15TH (GEE'S-JOHNSON'S) INFANTRY REGIMENT

*Organization:* Organized at Camden on January 2, 1862. Surrendered at Fort Donelson, Tennessee, on February 16, 1862. Declared exchanged in the fall of 1862. Reorganized at Jackson, Mississippi, on October 16, 1862. Field consolidation with the 16th Infantry Regiment from January or February 1863 to July 1863. Surrendered at Port Hudson, Louisiana, on July 8, 1863. Paroled later in month. Declared exchanged then reorganized in the fall of 1863. Field consolidation with the 19th Infantry Regiment from November 1863. Consolidated with the 15th, 20th and Dawson's-Hardy's Consolidated Infantry Regiment and designated as the 3rd Infantry Regiment Consolidated, Trans-Mississippi Department, on November 29, 1864. (There is some evidence that the consolidation had already occurred prior to September 30, 1864.)
*First Commander:* James M. Gee (Colonel)

*Field Officers:*  Benjamin W. Johnson (Colonel)
P. Lynch Lee (Major, Lieutenant Colonel)
Willim E. Stewart (Major)
John C. Wright (Lieutenant Colonel)

*Assignments:*  Fort Henry, Department #2 (January-February 1862)
Drake's Brigade, Fort Henry, Department #2 (February 1862)
Drake's Brigade, Johnson's Division, Fort Donelson, Department #2 (February 1862)
3rd Military District, Department of Mississippi and East Louisiana (November 1862)
Beall's Brigade, 3rd Military District, Department of Mississippi and East Louisiana (January-July 1863)

*Battles:*  Fort Henry (February 6, 1862)
Fort Donelson (February 12-16, 1862)
Port Hudson Siege (May-July 1863)

## 135.  ARKANSAS 15TH NORTHWEST (HOBBS'-BOONE'S) INFANTRY REGIMENT

*Organization:*  Organized by the change of designation of the 21st (McRae's) Infantry Regiment ca. February 1863. Regiment surrendered at Vicksburg, Mississippi, on July 4, 1863. Paroled there later in month. Consolidated with 14th, 16th and 21st Infantry Regiments and designated as the 1st Infantry Regiment Consolidated in January 1864.

*First Commander:*  James H. Hobbs (Colonel)

*Field Officers:*  Squire Boone (Lieutenant Colonel, Colonel)
William W. Reynolds (Lieutenant Colonel)
David A. Stuart (Major)

*Assignments:*  Green's Brigade, Price's-Forney's-Bowen's Division, Army of North Mississippi, Department of Mississippi and East Louisiana (February 1863)
Green's Brigade, Bowen's Division, 2nd Military District, Department of Mississippi and East Louisiana (April 1863)
Green's Brigade, Bowen's Division, Department of Mississippi and East Louisiana (May-July 1863)

*Battles:*  Vicksburg Campaign (May-July 1863)
Grand Gulf (April 29, 1863)
Port Gibson (May 1, 1863)
Champion Hill (May 16, 1863)
Big Black River Bridge (May 17, 1863)
Vicksburg Siege (May-July 1863)

## 136. ARKANSAS 16TH INFANTRY REGIMENT

*Organization:* Organized in Benton County on December 4, 1861. Companies had been mustered into Confederate service in October and November 1861. Reorganized at Corinth, Mississippi, on May 8, 1862. Field consolidation with the 14th, 17th, 18th and 23rd Infantry Regiments and the 8th Infantry Battalion in the winter of 1862-1863. Field consolidation with the 15th (Gee's-Johnson's) Infantry Regiment in the spring of 1863. Surrendered at Port Hudson, Louisiana, on July 8, 1863. Paroled later in month. Consolidated into two companies prior to September 30, 1864. Consolidated with the 14th, 15th Northwest and 21st Infantry Regiments and designated as the 1st Infantry Regiment Consolidated, Trans-Mississippi Department, in January 1864.

*First Commander:* John F. Hill (Colonel)
*Field Officers:* Samuel Farmer (Major)
William T. Neal (Lieutenant Colonel)
James M. Pittman (Major)
Benjamin T. Pixlee (Lieutenant Colonel)
David Provence (Colonel)
L. N. C. Swagerty (Major)
*Assignments:* McCulloch's Division, Department #2 (October-December 1861)
Hébert's Brigade, McCulloch's Division, Department #2 (December 1861-January 1862)
Hébert's Brigade, McCulloch's Division, Trans-Mississippi District, Department #2 (January-March 1862)
Hébert's Brigade, Price's Division, Trans-Mississippi District, Department #2 (March-April 1862)
Hébert's Brigade, Price's-Little's Division, Army of the West, Department #2 (April-September 1862)
Hébert's Brigade, Little's-Hébert's Division, Price's Corps, Army of West Tennessee, Department of Mississippi and East Louisiana (September-October 1862)
Hébert's Brigade, Bowen's Division, Price's Corps, Army of West Tennessee, Department of Mississippi and East Louisiana (October 1862)
Craven's Brigade, Bowen's Division, Price's Corps, Army of West Tennessee, Department of Mississippi and East Louisiana (October-December 1862)
Craven's Brigade, Bowen's Division, 2nd Corps, Army of North Mississippi, Department of Mississippi and East Louisiana (December 1862)
Beale's Brigade, 3rd Military District, Department of Mississippi and East Louisiana (January-July 1863)
*Battles:* Pea Ridge (March 7-8, 1862)
Corinth Campaign (April-June 1862)

Corinth (October 3-4, 1862)
Port Hudson Siege (May-July 1863)

## 137.   ARKANSAS 17TH INFANTRY BATTALION
*See:* ARKANSAS 17TH (LEMOYNE'S) INFANTRY REGIMENT

## 138.   ARKANSAS 17TH (LEMOYNE'S) INFANTRY REGIMENT
**Also Known As:**   Arkansas 17th Infantry Battalion
**Organization:**   Organized with eight companies at Fairfield, Yell County, on
August 1, 1861. Consolidated into six companies and consolidated with the
14th (McCarver's) Infantry Regiment and designated as the 21st Infantry
Regiment on May 14, 1862.
**First Commander:**   George W. Lemoyne (Colonel)
**Field Officers:**   John M. Dowdle (Major)
Lawrence (Major)
S. W. Williams (Lieutenant Colonel)
**Assignment:**   Rust's Brigade, Jones' Division, Army of the West, Department
#2 (April-May 1862)
**Battle:**   Corinth Campaign (April-June 1862)

## 139.   ARKANSAS 17TH (RECTOR'S-GRIFFITH'S) INFANTRY REGIMENT
**Organization:**   Organized on November 17, 1861. Reorganized at Tupelo,
Mississippi, on April 16, 1862. Portions of Companies A, B, C and G left west
of the Mississippi River became part of the 35th Infantry Regiment in early
1862. Field consolidation with the 14th, 16th, 18th and 23rd Infantry Regi-
ments and the 1st Infantry Battalion in January 1863. Consolidated with the
11th Infantry Regiment and designated as the 11th and 17th Infantry Regiment
Consolidated in January 1863.
**First Commander:**   Frank A. Rector (Colonel)
**Field Officers:**   Josephus Dotson (Lieutenant Colonel)
John Griffith (Lieutenant Colonel, Colonel)
Benjamin J. Jett (Major)
Walter H. Matheson (Major)
**Assignments:**   McCulloch's Division, Department #2 (December 1861)
Hébert's Brigade, McCulloch's Division, Department #2 (December 1861-Jan-
uary 1862)
Hébert's Brigade, McCulloch's Division, Trans-Mississippi District, Depart-
ment #2 (January-March 1862)
Little's Brigade, Price's Division, Trans-Mississippi District, Department #2
· (March-April 1862)

Hébert's Brigade, Price's-Little's Division, Army of the West, Department #2 (April-September 1862)

Hébert's Brigade, Little's Division, 1st Corps, Price's Corps, Army of West Tennessee, Department of Mississippi and East Louisiana (September-October 1862)

Hébert's Brigade, Bowen's Division, Price's Corps, 1st Corps, Army of West Tennessee, Department of Mississippi and East Louisiana (October 1862)

Craven's Brigade, Bowen's Division, 1st Corps, Price's Corps, Army of West Tennessee, Department of Mississippi and East Louisiana (October-December 1862)

Craven's Brigade, Bowen's Division, 2nd Corps, Army of North Mississippi, Department of Mississippi and East Louisiana (December 1862)

Beale's Brigade, 3rd Military District, Department of Mississippi and East Louisiana (January-July 1863)

**Battles:** Pea Ridge (March 7-8, 1862)

Corinth Campaign (April-June 1862)

Iuka (September 19, 1862)

Corinth (October 3-4, 1862)


## 140. ARKANSAS 18TH INFANTRY BATTALION

*See:* ARKANSAS 14TH (MCCARVER'S) INFANTRY REGIMENT


## 141. ARKANSAS 18TH (CARROLL'S-DALY'S-CROCKETT'S) INFANTRY REGIMENT

**Organization:** Organized at Devall's Bluff on April 2, 1862. Field consolidation with the 14th, 16th, 17th and 23rd Infantry Regiments and the 8th Infantry Battalion in January 1863. Field consolidation with the 14th and 23rd Infantry Regiments from February 1863 to July 8, 1863. Surrendered at Port Hudson, Louisiana, on July 8, 1863. Paroled later in month. Mounted at some time prior to April 20, 1864. Surrendered by General E. Kirby Smith, commanding the Trans-Mississippi Department, on May 26, 1865.

**First Commander:** D. W. Carroll (Colonel)

**Field Officers:** Robert H. Crockett (Major, Lieutenant Colonel, Colonel)

John N. Daly (Lieutenant Colonel, Colonel)

W. N. Parrish (Lieutenant Colonel)

Samuel H. Sutherland (Major)

**Assignments:** Rust's-Dockery's Brigade, Jones'-Maury's Division, Army of the West, Department #2 (April-September 1862)

Cabell's Brigade, Maury's Division, Price's Corps, Army of West Tennessee, Department of Mississippi and East Louisiana (September-October 1862)

Craven's Brigade, Bowen's Division, Price's Corps, Army of West Tennessee, Department of Mississippi and East Louisiana (October-December 1862)

Craven's Brigade, Bowen's Division, 2nd Corps, Army of North Mississippi, Department of Mississippi and East Louisiana (December 1862)

Beall's Brigade, 3rd Military District, Department of Mississippi and East Louisiana (January-July 1863 )

Dockery's Brigade, Fagan's Cavalry Division, District of Arkansas, Trans-Mississippi Department (April 1864)

**Battles:** Corinth Campaign (April-June 1862)

Port Hudson Siege (May-July 1863)

Camden Expedition (March-May 1864)

Marks' Mill (April 25, 1864)

## 142. ARKANSAS 18TH (MARMADUKE'S) INFANTRY REGIMENT

**Organization:** Organized by the addition of two companies to the 1st Infantry Battalion in December 1861. Designation changed to 3rd Confederate Infantry Regiment on January 31, 1862, per S.O. #25, Adjutant and Inspector General's Office.

**First Commander:** Jonathan S. Marmaduke (Colonel)

**Field Officer:** James B. Johnson (Lieutenant Colonel)

**Assignment:** Hindman's Brigade, Hardee's Division, Central Army of Kentucky, Department #2 (December 1861-January 1862)

## 143. ARKANSAS 19TH (DAWSON'S) INFANTRY REGIMENT

**Organization:** Organized and mustered into Confederate service for 12 months at Nashville, Arkansas, on November 21, 1861. Reorganized on August 13, 1862. Much of the regiment surrendered at Arkansas Post on January 11, 1863. Portion not captured was consolidated with parts of Crawford's Infantry Battalion and the 24th Infantry Regiment and designated as Dawson's-Hardy's Infantry Regiment Consolidated in early 1863. Balance of the regiment paroled and declared exchanged in late 1863. Field consolidation with the 8th Infantry Regiment from November 15, 1863, to April 9, 1865. Consolidated with 1st, 2nd, 5th, 6th, 7th, 8th, 13th, 15th and 24th Infantry Regiments and the 3rd Confederate Infantry Regiment and designated as the 1st Infantry Regiment Consolidated at Smithfield, North Carolina, on April 9, 1865.

**First Commander:** Charles L. Dawson (Colonel)

**Field Officers:** James Anderson (Major)

David H. Hamiter (Major)

Augustus S. Hutchison (Lieutenant Colonel, Major)

John G. McKean (Major)

P. R. Smith (Lieutenant Colonel)

**Assignments:** Unattached, Trans-Mississippi District, Department #2 (March-May 1862)

Department of the Indian Territory (May-June 1862)

Dunnington's Brigade, Churchill's Brigade, District of Arkansas, Trans-Mississippi Department (August 1862-January 1863)

Liddell's Brigade, Cleburne's Division, 2nd Corps, Army of Tennessee (November 1863)

Liddell's-Govan's Brigade, Cleburne's-Brown's Division, 1st Corps, Army of Tennessee (November 1863-April 1865)

**Battles:** Pea Ridge (March 7-8, 1862)

Arkansas Post (January 4-11, 1863)

Chattanooga Siege (September-November 1863)

Chattanooga (November 23-25, 1863)

Ringgold Gap (November 27, 1863)

Atlanta Campaign (May-September 1864)

Dalton (May 5-11, 1864)

Resaca (May 14-15, 1864)

New Hope Church (May 25-June 4, 1864)

Pickett's Mill (May 27, 1864)

Kennesaw Mountain (June 27, 1864)

Peach Tree Creek (July 20, 1864)

Atlanta (July 22, 1864)

Atlanta Siege (July-September 1864)

Jonesboro (August 31-September 1, 1864)

Franklin (November 30, 1864)

Nashville (December 15-16, 1864)

Carolinas Campaign (February-April 1865)

Bentonville (March 19-21, 1865)


## 144. ARKANSAS 19TH (SMEAD'S-DOCKERY'S) INFANTRY REGIMENT

**Organization:** Organized at Devall's Bluff on April 3, 1862. Reorganized on May 12, 1862. Regiment surrendered at Vicksburg, Mississippi, on July 4, 1863. Paroled there later in month. Mounted prior to April 20, 1864. Disappears from the records in 1864 but possibly merged into the 3rd Infantry Regiment Consolidated.

**First Commander:** Hamilton P. Smead (Colonel)

**Field Officers:** W. H. Dismukes (Lieutenant Colonel)

Thomas P. Dockery (Colonel)

H. G. P. Williams (Major)

*Assignments:* Rust's-Dockery's Brigade, Jones'-Maury's Division, Army of the West, Department #2 (April-September 1862)

Cabell's Brigade, Maury's Division, Price's Corps, Army of West Tennessee, Department of Mississippi and East Louisiana (September-October 1862)

Craven's Brigade, Bowen's Division, 2nd Corps, Army of West Tennessee, Department of Mississippi and East Louisiana (October-December 1862)

Craven's Brigade, Bowen's Division, 2nd Corps, Army of North Mississippi, Department of Mississippi and East Louisiana (December 1862-January 1863)

Green's Brigade, Price's Division, Army of North Mississippi, Department of Mississippi and East Louisiana (January 1863)

Green's Brigade, Forney's-Bowen's Division, 2nd Military District, Department of Mississippi and East Louisiana (April 1863)

Green's Brigade, Bowen's Division, Department of Mississippi and East Louisiana (April-July 1863)

Dockery's Brigade, Fagan's Cavalry Division, District of Arkansas, Trans-Mississippi Department (April 1864)

*Battles:* Corinth Campaign (April-June 1862)

Corinth (October 3-4, 1862)

Vicksburg Campaign (May-July 1863)

Port Gibson (May 1, 1863)

Champion Hill (May 16, 1863)

Big Black River Bridge (May 17, 1863)

Vicksburg Siege (May-July 1863)

Camden Expedition (March-May 1864)

Marks' Mill (April 25, 1864)


## 145.   ARKANSAS 20TH INFANTRY REGIMENT

*Organization:* Organized by the change of designation of the 22nd Infantry Regiment on May 13, 1862. Regiment surrendered at Vicksburg, Mississippi, on July 4, 1863. Paroled there later in month. Declared exchanged in late 1863. Mounted at some time prior to April 20, 1864. Consolidated with the 15th and Dawson's-Hardy's Consolidated Infantry Regiments and designated the 3rd Infantry Regiment Consolidated on November 29, 1864. (There is some evidence that this consolidation occurred prior to September 30, 1864.)

*First Commander:* Henry P. Johnson (Colonel)

*Field Officers:* James H. Fletcher (Lieutenant Colonel, Colonel)

William S. Haven (Major)

Daniel W. Jones (Major, Colonel)

W. R. Kelley (Lieutenant Colonel)

J. W. Long (Major)

H. G. Robertson (Lieutenant Colonel, Major)

**Assignments:** Rust's-Dockery's-Cabell's Brigade, Jones'-Maury's Division, Army of the West, Department #2 (April-September 1862)

Cabell's Brigade, Maury's Division, Price's Corps, Army of West Tennessee, Department of Mississippi and East Louisiana (September-October 1862)

Craven's Brigade, Bowen's Division, 2nd Corps, Army of West Tennessee, Department of Mississippi and East Louisiana (October-December 1862)

Craven's Brigade, Bowen's Division, 2nd Corps, Army of North Mississippi, Department of Mississippi and East Louisiana (December 1862-January 1863)

Green's Brigade, Price's Division, Army of North Mississippi, Department of Mississippi and East Louisiana (January 1863)

Green's Brigade, Forney's-Bowen's Division, 2nd Military District, Department of Mississippi and East Louisiana (April 1863)

Green's Brigade, Bowen's Division, Department of Mississippi and East Louisiana (April-July 1863)

Dockery's Brigade, Fagan's Cavalry Division, District of Arkansas, Trans-Mississippi Department (April 1864)

**Battles:** Corinth Campaign (April-June 1862)

Farmington (May 1862)

Corinth (October 3-4, 1862)

Coffeeville (December 15, 1862)

Vicksburg Campaign (May-July 1863)

Grand Gulf (April 29, 1863)

Port Gibson (May 1, 1863)

Champion Hill (May 16, 1863)

Big Black River Bridge (May 17, 1863)

Vicksburg Siege (May-July 1863)

Camden Expedition (March-May 1864)

Marks' Mill (April 25, 1864)

## 146.   ARKANSAS 21ST INFANTRY REGIMENT

**Organization:** Organized by the consolidation of the 14th (McCarver's) and 17th (Lemoyne's) Infantry Battalions on May 14, 1862. Regiment surrendered at Vicksburg, Mississippi, on July 4, 1863. Paroled there later in month. Declared exchanged on September 12, 1863. Consolidated with the 14th (Mitchell's-Powers'), 15th Northwest and 16th Infantry Regiments and designated the 1st Infantry Regiment Consolidated, Trans-Mississippi Department, in January 1864.

**First Commander:** Jordan E. Cravens (Colonel)

**Field Officers:** William M. Dowdle (Major)

William G. Matheny (Lieutenant Colonel)

Harrison Moore (Major)

**Assignments:** Rust's Brigade, Jones' Division, Army of the West, Department #2 (May 1862)

Dockery's-Cabell's Brigade, Maury's Division, Price's Corps, Army of the West, Department #2 (June-September 1862)

Cabell's Brigade, Maury's Division, 1st Corps, Army of the West, Department of Mississippi and East Louisiana (September-October 1862)

Craven's Brigade, Bowen's Division, 2nd Corps, Army of North Mississippi, Department of Mississippi and East Louisiana (December 1862)

Green's Brigade, Price's Division, Army of North Mississippi, Department of Mississippi and East Louisiana (January 1863)

Green's Brigade, Price's-Forney's-Bowen's Division, 2nd Military District, Department of Mississippi and East Louisiana (April 1863)

Green's Brigade, Bowen's Division, Department of Mississippi and East Louisiana (April-July 1863)

**Battles:** Corinth Campaign (April-June 1862)

Corinth (October 3-4, 1862)

Grand Gulf (April 29, 1863)

Vicksburg Campaign (May-July 1863)

Port Gibson (May 1, 1863)

Champion Hill (May 16, 1863)

Big Black River Bridge (May 17, 1863)

Vicksburg Siege (May-July 1863)


### 147.   ARKANSAS 21ST INFANTRY REGIMENT MILITIA

**Organization:** Undated descriptive list for six companies are the only record of this unit.

**First Commander:** Robert Query (Colonel)


### 148.   ARKANSAS 21ST (MCRAE'S) INFANTRY BATTALION

**Organization:** Organized by the increasing of the 3rd Infantry Battalion to a regiment on December 3, 1861. Reorganized on May 8, 1862. Designation changed to the 15th Northwest (Hobbs'-Boone's) Infantry Regiment ca. February 1863.

**First Commander:** Dandridge McRae (Colonel)

**Field Officers:** Squire Boone (Lieutenant Colonel)

James H. Hobbs (Lieutenant Colonel, Colonel)

William Thompson (Major)

**Assignments:** McCulloch's Division, Department #2 (December 1861)

Hébert's Brigade, McCulloch's Division, Department #2 (December 1861-January 1862)

Hébert's Brigade, McCulloch's Division, Trans-Mississippi District, Department #2 (January-March 1862)

Hébert's Brigade, Price's Division, Trans-Mississippi District, Department #2 (March-April 1862)

Hébert's Brigade, Price's-Little's Division, Army of the West, Department #2 (April-September 1862)

Hébert's Brigade, Little's-Hébert's Division, Price's Corps, Army of West Tennessee, Department of Mississippi and East Louisiana (September-October 1862)

Hébert's Brigade, Bowen's Division, Price's Corps, Army of West Tennessee, Department of Mississippi and East Louisiana (October 1862)

Craven's Brigade, Bowen's Division, Price's Corps, Army of West Tennessee, Department of Mississippi and East Louisiana (October-December 1862)

Craven's Brigade, Bowen's Division, 2nd Corps, Army of North Mississippi, Department of Mississippi and East Louisiana (December 1862)

Green's Brigade, 2nd Price's Division, Army of North Mississippi, Department of Mississippi and East Louisiana (January-February 1863)

**Battles:** Pea Ridge (March 7-8, 1862)
Corinth Campaign (April-June 1862)

## 149. ARKANSAS 22ND INFANTRY REGIMENT

*Organization:* Organized in February or March 1862. Designation changed to the 20th Infantry Regiment on May 13, 1862.

*First Commander:* George W. King (Colonel)
*Field Officers:* Alf Carrigan (Lieutenant Colonel)
James H. Fletcher (Major)

*Assignments:* Unattached, Trans-Mississippi District, Department #2 (March 1862)
Rust's Brigade, Jones' Division, Army of the West, Department #2 (April-May 1862)

*Battles:* Pea Ridge (March 7-8, 1862)
Fort Pillow (April-June 1862)
Corinth Campaign (April-June 1862)

## 150. ARKANSAS 22ND (RECTOR'S-KING'S-MCCORD'S) INFANTRY REGIMENT

*See:* ARKANSAS 35TH INFANTRY REGIMENT

## 151.  ARKANSAS 23RD INFANTRY REGIMENT

*Organization:*  Organized by the consolidation of Adams' and Hughes' Infantry Battalions and Adair's Infantry Company on April 25, 1862. Companies reorganized on May 27, 1862, but the regiment itself was not organized until September 10, 1862. Field consolidation with the 14th and 18th Infantry Regiments in early 1863. Surrendered at Port Hudson, Louisiana, on July 8, 1863. Paroled later in month. Mounted in mid-1864. Surrendered by Brigadier General M. Jeff. Thompson, commanding Northern Sub-district of Arkansas, District of Arkansas and West Louisiana, Trans-Mississippi Department, on May 11, 1865.

*First Commander:*  Charles W. Adams (Colonel)
*Field Officers:*  Erastus L. Black (Major, Lieutenant Colonel)
Simon P. Hughes (Lieutenant Colonel)
Oliver P. Lyles (Colonel)
A. A. Pennington (Major, Lieutenant Colonel)
*Assignments:*  Maury's-Moore's Brigade, Jones'-Maury's Division, Army of the West, Department #2 (April-September 1862)
Moore's Brigade, Maury's Division, Price's Corps, Army of West Tennessee, Department of Mississippi and East Louisiana (September-October 1862)
Craven's Brigade, Bowen's Division, Price's Corps, Army of West Tennessee, Department of Mississippi and East Louisiana (October-December 1862)
Craven's Brigade, Bowen's Division, 2nd Corps, Army of North Mississippi, Department of Mississippi and East Louisiana (December 1862)
Beall's Brigade, 3rd Military District, Department of Mississippi and East Louisiana (January-July 1863)
Unattached, Fagan's Cavalry Division, District of Arkansas, Trans-Mississippi Department (August-September 1864)
Unattached, Fagan's Cavalry Division, Army of Missouri, Trans-Mississippi Department, (September-December 1864)
Army of the Northern Sub-District of Arkansas, District of Arkansas, Trans-Mississippi Department (April 1865)
Army of the Northern Sub-District of Arkansas, District of Arkansas and West Louisiana, Trans-Mississippi Department (April-May 1865)
*Battles:*  Corinth Campaign (April-June 1862)
Corinth (October 3-4, 1862)
Port Hudson Siege (May-July 1863)
Price's Missouri Raid (September-October 1864)

## 152.  ARKANSAS 24TH INFANTRY REGIMENT

*Organization:*  Organized on June 6, 1862. Much of the regiment surrendered at Arkansas Post on January 11, 1863. Portion not captured there consolidated with Crawford's Infantry Battalion and the 19th (Dawson's) Infantry Regiment and designated as Dawson's-Hardy's Infantry Regiment Consolidated in early 1863. Balance of the regiment paroled and declared exchanged at City Point, Virginia, in May 1863. Consolidated into a battalion of two companies on November 16, 1863. Field consolidation with the 2nd Infantry Regiment from November 16, 1863, to early 1865. Additional field consolidation with the 15th Infantry Regiment from November 16, 1863, to early 1864. Additional field consolidation with the 1st, 2nd, 5th, 13th and 15th Infantry Regiments from December 1864 to early 1865. New field consolidation with the 15th Infantry Regiment and the 3rd Confederate Infantry Regiment in early 1865. Consolidated with 1st, 2nd, 5th, 6th, 7th, 8th, 13th, 15th and 19th (Dawson's) Infantry Regiments and designated as the 1st Infantry Regiment Consolidated at Smithfield, North Carolina, on April 9, 1865.

**First Commander:**   Edward E. Portlock, Jr. (Colonel)

**Field Officers:**   William R. Hardy (Major)
Thomas M. Whittington (Lieutenant Colonel)
Francis H. Wood (Major)

**Assignments:**   Unattached, Churchill's Division, District of Arkansas, Trans-
   Mississippi Department (detachment) (December 1862-January 1863)
Liddell's Brigade, Cleburne's Division, 2nd Corps, Army of Tennessee (Novem-
   ber 1863)
Liddell's-Govan's Brigade, Cleburne's-Brown's Division, 1st Corps, Army of
   Tennessee (November 1863-April 1865)

**Battles:**   Arkansas Post (detachment) (January 4-11, 1863)
Chattanooga Siege (September-November 1863)
Chattanooga (November 23-25, 1863)
Ringgold Gap (November 27, 1863)
Atlanta Campaign (May-September 1864)
Dalton (May 5-11, 1864)
Resaca (May 14-15, 1864)
New Hope Church (May 25-June 4, 1864)
Kennesaw Mountain (June 27, 1864)
Peach Tree Creek (July 20, 1864)
Atlanta (July 22, 1864)
Atlanta Siege (July-September 1864)
Jonesboro (August 31-September 1, 1864)
Franklin (November 30, 1864)
Nashville (December 15-16, 1864)
Carolinas Campaign (February-April 1865)
Bentonville (March 19-21, 1865)

## 153.   ARKANSAS 25TH INFANTRY REGIMENT

*Also Known As:*   30th Infantry Regiment (until January 1863)

*Organization:*   Organized by increasing the 11th Infantry Battalion to a regiment on June 18, 1862. Consolidated with the 1st and 2nd Mounted Rifles Regiments, 4th Infantry Battalion and the 4th and 9th Infantry Regiment and designated as the 1st Mounted Rifles Regiment Consolidated at Smithfield, North Carolina, on April 9, 1865.

*First Commander:*   Charles J. Turnbull (Colonel)

*Field Officers:*   James J. Franklin (Major)
Eli Hufstedler (Lieutenant Colonel)
L. L. Noles (Major)
Thomas S. Simington (Lieutenant Colonel)

*Assignments:*   Churchill's Brigade, McCown's Division, Army of the West, Department #2 (June-July 1862)
McNair's Brigade, McCown's Division, Department of East Tennessee (July-December 1862)
McNair's Brigade, McCown's Division, E. K. Smith's Corps, Army of Tennessee (December 1862-March 1863)
McNair's Brigade, McCown's Division, 1st Corps, Army of Tennessee (March-April 1863)
McNair's Brigade, Walker's Division, Department of the West (June 1863)
McNair's Brigade, French's Division, Department of the West (June-July 1863)
McNair's Brigade, French's Division, Department of Mississippi and East Louisiana (July-September 1863)
McNair's Brigade, Johnson's Provisional Division, Army of Tennessee (September 1863)
McNair's Brigade, French's Division, Department of Mississippi and East Louisiana (September 1863-January 1864)
McNair's Brigade, French's Division, Department of Alabama, Mississippi and East Louisiana (January-February 1864)
McNair's-D. H. Reynolds' Brigade, Department of the Gulf (February-April 1864)
D. H. Reynolds' Brigade, District of the Gulf, Department of Alabama, Mississippi and East Louisiana (April-May 1864)
D. H. Reynolds' Brigade, Cantey's-Walthall's Division, Army of Mississippi (May-July 1864)
D. H. Reynolds' Brigade, Walthall's Division, 3rd Corps, Army of Tennessee (July 1864-April 1865)

*Battles:*   Richmond, Kentucky (August 29-30, 1862)
Perryville (October 8, 1862)
Murfreesboro (December 31, 1862-January 3, 1863)

Jackson Siege (July 1863)
Chickamauga (September 19-20, 1863)
Chattanooga Siege (September-November 1863)
Atlanta Campaign (May-September 1864)
Dug Gap (May 8, 1864)
Resaca (May 14-15, 1864)
New Hope Church (May 25-June 4, 1864)
Kennesaw Mountain (June 27, 1864)
Moore's Hill (July 19, 1864)
Peach Tree Creek (July 20, 1864)
Atlanta (July 22, 1864)
Ezra Church (July 28, 1864)
Atlanta Siege (July-September 1864)
Jonesboro (August 31-September 1, 1864)
Lovejoy's Station (September 2-5, 1864)
Moon's Station (October 3, 1864)
Franklin (November 30, 1864)
Nashville (December 15-16, 1864)
Sugar Creek (December 26, 1864)
Carolinas Campaign (February-April 1865)
Averasboro (March 16, 1865)
Bentonville (March 19-21, 1865)

### 154.  ARKANSAS 26TH INFANTRY REGIMENT

*Also Known As:*  Arkansas 3rd Trans-Mississippi Infantry Regiment

*Organization:*  Organized by the increase of Morgan's Infantry Battalion to a regiment on July 23, 1862. Surrendered by General E. Kirby Smith, commanding the Trans-Mississippi Department, on May 26, 1865.

*First Commander:*  Asa S. Morgan (Colonel)

*Field Officers:*  Iverson L. Brooks (Lieutenant Colonel, Colonel)
Samuel Gibson (Major)
James P. Stanley (Major, Lieutenant Colonel)
John C. Wright (Lieutenant Colonel)
Fountain P. Yell (Major, Lieutenant Colonel, Colonel)

*Assignments:*  McRae's Brigade, Hindman's Division, Trans-Mississippi Department (January-February 1863)
McRae's-Churchill's Brigade, Price's Division, District of Arkansas, Trans-Mississippi Department (April 1863-March 1864)
Churchill's-Gause's Brigade, Arkansas Division, District of Arkansas, Trans-Mississippi Department (March-April 1864)

Gause's Brigade, Arkansas Division, Detachment from District of Arkansas, District of West Louisiana, Trans-Mississippi Department (April 1864)

Gause's Brigade, Arkansas Division, District of Arkansas, Trans-Mississippi Department (April-September 1864)

1st (Roane's) Arkansas Brigade, 1st (Churchill's) Arkansas Division, 2nd Corps, Trans-Mississippi Department (September 1864-May 1865)

**Battles:** Devil's Backbone (September 1, 1863)

Little Rock (September 10, 1863)

Red River Campaign (March-May 1864)

Jenkins' Ferry (April 30, 1864)

## 155. ARKANSAS 27TH INFANTRY REGIMENT

*Organization:* Organized for the war in July 1862. Surrendered by General E. Kirby Smith, commanding the Trans-Mississippi Department, on May 26, 1865.

*First Commander:* James R. Shaler (Colonel)

*Field Officers:* Beal Gaither (Major, Colonel)

Arthur J. Magenis (Lieutenant Colonel)

James M. Riggs (Lieutenant Colonel)

*Assignments:* Shaver's Brigade, Hindman's Division, 1st Corps, Trans-Mississippi Department (January-February 1863)

Tappan's Brigade, Price's Division, District of Arkansas, Trans-Mississippi Department (April-November 1863)

Drayton's Brigade, Price's Division, District of Arkansas, Trans-Mississippi Department (January-March 1864)

Tappan's Brigade, Arkansas Division, District of Arkansas, Trans-Mississippi Department (March-April 1864)

Tappan's Brigade, Arkansas Division, Detachment from District of Arkansas, District of West Louisiana, Trans-Mississippi Department (April 1864)

Tappan's Brigade, Arkansas Division, District of Arkansas, Trans-Mississippi Department (April-September 1864)

3rd (Tappan's) Arkansas Brigade, 1st (Churchill's) Arkansas Division, 2nd Corps, Trans-Mississippi Department (September 1864-May 1865)

**Battles:** Little Rock (September 10, 1863)

Red River Campaign (March-May 1864)

Jenkins' Ferry (April 30, 1864)

## 156. ARKANSAS 28TH INFANTRY REGIMENT

*See:* ARKANSAS 36TH INFANTRY REGIMENT

## 157. ARKANSAS 29TH INFANTRY REGIMENT

*See:* ARKANSAS 37TH INFANTRY REGIMENT

## 158.  ARKANSAS 30TH INFANTRY REGIMENT

*Also Known As:*  Arkansas 39th Infantry Regiment
Arkansas 5th Trans-Mississippi Infantry Regiment
*Organization:*  Organized ca. June 18, 1862. Field consolidation with the 32nd
Infantry Regiment from December 1863 to early 1864. Field consolidation with
Dawson's Infantry Regiment. Consolidated in April 1864. Surrendered by
General E. Kirby Smith, commanding the Trans-Mississippi Department, on
May 26, 1865.
*First Commander:*  Archibald J. McNeill (Colonel)
*Field Officers:*  Casten W. Baldwin (Lieutenant Colonel)
Paul M. Cobbs (Major, Lieutenant Colonel)
Martin Dawson (Major)
Robert A. Hart (Lieutenant Colonel, Colonel)
Joseph C. Martin (Major)
James W. Rogan (Major, Lieutenant Colonel, Colonel)
*Assignments:*  McRae's Brigade, Hindman's Division, Trans-Mississippi De-
partment (January-February 1863)
McRae's-Churchill's Brigade, Price's Division, District of Arkansas, Trans-Mis-
sissippi Department (April 1863-March 1864)
Tappan's Brigade, Arkansas Division, Detachment from District of Arkansas,
District of West Louisiana, Trans-Mississippi Department (April 1864)
Tappan's Brigade, Arkansas Division, District of Arkansas, Trans-Mississippi
Department (April 1864)
1st (Roane's) Arkansas Brigade, 1st (Churchill's) Arkansas Division, 2nd
Corps, Trans-Mississippi Department (September 1864-May 1865)
*Battles:*  Helena (July 4, 1863)
Little Rock (September 10, 1863)
Red River Campaign (March-May 1864)
Jenkins' Ferry (April 30, 1864)

## 159.  ARKANSAS 30TH (TURNBULL'S) INFANTRY REGIMENT

*See:*  ARKANSAS 25TH INFANTRY REGIMENT

## 160.  ARKANSAS 31ST INFANTRY REGIMENT

*Organization:*  Organized by the addition of Company G, Williamson's Infantry Battalion, to McCray's Infantry Battalion on May 27, 1862. Field consolidation with the 25th Infantry Regiment from March 1863 to the summer of
1863. Field consolidation with the 4th Infantry Regiment and the 4th Infantry
Battalion from the summer of 1863 to January 1864. Field consolidation with
the 25th Infantry Regiment from January 1864. No record after January 20,
1864.

*First Commander:* Thomas H. McCray (Colonel)
*Field Officers:* J. W. Clark (Major)
Davis G. Daugherty (Major)
Jesse L. Hays (Lieutenant Colonel)
John A. Jacoway (Lieutenant Colonel)
James F. Johnson (Lieutenant Colonel)
James M. Morgan (Major)
*Assignments:* Hogg's Brigade, McCown's Division, Army of the West, Department #2 (May-June 1862)
McNair's Brigade, McCown's Division, Department of East Tennessee (July-August 1862)
McNair's Brigade, McCown's Division, Army of Kentucky, Department #2 (August-October 1862)
McNair's Brigade, McCown's Division, E. K. Smith's Corps, Army of Tennessee (November 1862-March 1863)
McNair's Brigade, McCown's Division, 1st Corps, Army of Tennessee (March-April 1863)
McNair's Brigade, Walker's Division, Department of the West (June 1863)
McNair's Brigade, French's Division, Department of the West (June-July 1863)
McNair's Brigade, French's Division, Department of Mississippi and East Louisiana (July-August 1863)
McNair's Brigade, Johnson's Provisional Division, Army of Tennessee (September 1863)
McNair's Brigade, French's Division, Department of Mississippi and East Louisiana (September 1863-January 1864)
*Battles:* Murfreesboro (December 31, 1862-January 3, 1863)
Jackson Siege (July 1863)
Chickamauga (September 19-20, 1863)
Chattanooga Siege (September-November 1863)

## 161. ARKANSAS 32ND INFANTRY REGIMENT

*Also Known As:* Arkansas 4th Trans-Mississippi Infantry Regiment
*Organization:* Organized for three years or the war by increasing of Matlock's Cavalry Battalion to a regiment on August 6, 1862. Reorganized on December 1, 1863. Field consolidation with the 30th Infantry Regiment from December 1863 to some time in 1864. Surrendered by General E. Kirby Smith, commanding the Trans-Mississippi Department, on May 26, 1865.
*First Commander:* Charles H. Matlock (Colonel)
*Field Officers:* Lucian C. Gause (Major, Colonel)
William Hicks (Lieutenant Colonel)
Arthur F. Stephenson (Major)

Charles L. Young (Major, Lieutenant Colonel)

**Assignments:** McRae's Brigade, Hindman's Division, Trans-Mississippi Department (January-February 1863)
McRae's-Churchill's Brigade, Price's Division, District of Arkansas, Trans-Mississippi Department (April 1863-March 1864)
Tappan's Brigade, Arkansas Division, Detachment from District of Arkansas, District of West Louisiana, Trans-Mississippi Department (April 1864)
Tappan's Brigade, Arkansas Division, District of Arkansas, Trans-Mississippi Department (April 1864)
1st (Roane's) Arkansas Brigade, 1st (Churchill's) Arkansas Division, 2nd Corps, Trans-Mississippi Department (September 1864-May 1865)

**Battles:** Helena (July 4, 1863)
Little Rock (September 10, 1863)
Red River Campaign (March-May 1864)
Jenkins' Ferry (April 30, 1864)

## 162. ARKANSAS 33RD INFANTRY REGIMENT

**Organization:** Organized on July 11, 1862. Surrendered by General E. Kirby Smith, commanding the Trans-Mississippi Department, on May 26, 1865.

**First Commander:** H. L. Grinstead (Colonel)

**Field Officers:** W. L. Crenshaw (Major)
H. W. McMillan (Lieutenant Colonel)
William T. Steele, (Major)
Thomas D. Thomson (Lieutenant Colonel)

**Assignments:** Shaver's Brigade, Hindman's Division, Trans-Mississippi Department (January-February 1863)
Tappan's Brigade, Price's Division, District of Arkansas, Trans-Mississippi Department (April-November 1863)
Drayton's Brigade, Price's Division, District of Arkansas, Trans-Mississippi Department (January-March 1864)
Tappan's Brigade, Arkansas Division, District of Arkansas, Trans-Mississippi Department (March-April 1864)
Tappan's Brigade, Arkansas Division, Detachment from District of Arkansas, District of West Louisiana, Trans-Mississippi Department (April 1864)
3rd (Tappan's) Arkansas Brigade, 1st (Churchill's) Arkansas Division, 2nd Corps, Trans-Mississippi Department (April 1864-May 1865)

**Battles:** Little Rock (September 10, 1863)
Red River Campaign (March-May 1864)
Jenkins' Ferry (April 30, 1864)

## 163. ARKANSAS 34TH INFANTRY REGIMENT

*Also Known As:* Arkansas 2nd (Brook's) Infantry Regiment
*Organization:* Organized by companies between June and August 1862. Regiment organized on August 16, 1862. Surrendered by General E. Kirby Smith, commanding the Trans-Mississippi Department, on May 26, 1865.
*First Commander:* William H. Brooks (Colonel)
*Field Officers:* F. R. Earle (Major)
Thomas M. Gunter (Lieutenant Colonel)
James R. Pettigrew (Major, Lieutenant Colonel)
*Assignments:* Fagan's Brigade, Hindman's Division, Trans-Mississippi Department (January-February 1863)
Fagan's Brigade, Price's Division, District of Arkansas, Trans-Mississippi Department (April-November 1863)
Fagan's-Hawthorn's Brigade, District of Arkansas, Trans-Mississippi Department (January-April 1864)
Hawthorn's Brigade, Arkansas Division, District of Arkansas, Trans-Mississippi Department (April 1864)
4th (Hawthorn's) Arkansas Brigade, 1st (Churchill's) Arkansas Division, 2nd Corps, Trans-Mississippi Department (April 1864-May 1865)
*Battles:* Helena (July 4, 1863)
Little Rock (September 10, 1863)
Jenkins' Ferry (April 30, 1864)
Ivey's Ford (January 17, 1865)

## 164. ARKANSAS 35TH INFANTRY REGIMENT

*Also Known As:* Arkansas 22nd (Rector's-King's-McCord's) Infantry Regiment
Arkansas 1st (Rector's) Infantry Regiment, Northwest Division
*Organization:* Organized by companies in June 1862. Regiment organized on July 11, 1862. Surrendered by General E. Kirby Smith, commanding the Trans-Mississippi Department, on May 26, 1865.
*First Commander:* Frank A. Rector (Colonel)
*Field Officers:* John J. Dillard (Major)
James P. King (Colonel)
Harry J. McCord (Lieutenant Colonel, Colonel)
Mark T. Tatum (Major)
John W. Wallace (Lieutenant Colonel)
*Assignments:* Fagan's Brigade, Hindman's Division, Trans-Mississippi Department (January-February 1863)
Fagan's Brigade, Price's Division, District of Arkansas, Trans-Mississippi Department (April-November 1863)

Fagan's-Hawthorn's Brigade, District of Arkansas, Trans-Mississippi Department (January-April 1864)

Hawthorn's Brigade, Arkansas Division, District of Arkansas, Trans-Mississippi Department (April 1864)

4th (Hawthorn's) Arkansas Brigade, 1st (Churchill's) Arkansas Division, 2nd Corps, Trans-Mississippi Department (September 1864-May 1865)

**Battles:**  Helena (July 4, 1863)
Little Rock (September 10, 1863)
Jenkins' Ferry (April 30, 1864)

## 165.   ARKANSAS 36TH INFANTRY REGIMENT

**Also Known As:**  Arkansas 28th Infantry Regiment (in 1862)
Arkansas 2nd Trans-Mississippi Infantry Regiment

**Organization:**  Organized by companies in June 1862. Regiment organzied in June or July 1862. Consolidated into five companies on September 30, 1863. Surrendered by General E. Kirby Smith, commanding the Trans-Mississippi Department, on May 26, 1865.

**First Commander:**  Dandridge McRae (Colonel)

**Field Officers:**  James M. Davie (Colonel)
John E. Glenn (Major, Lieutenant Colonel)
W. S. Hanna (Major, Lieutenant Colonel)
Joseph F. Hathaway (Major)
Walter C. Robinson (Lieutenant Colonel)

**Assignments:**  McRae's Brigade, Hindman's Division, Trans-Mississippi Department (January-February 1863)

McRae's-Churchill's Brigade, Price's Division, District of Arkansas, Trans-Mississippi Department (April 1862-March 1864)

Churchill's-Gause's Brigade, Arkansas Division, District of Arkansas, Trans-Mississippi Department (March-April 1864)

Gause's Brigade, Arkansas Division, Detachment from District of Arkansas, District of West Louisiana, Trans-Mississippi Department (April 1864)

Gause's Brigade, Arkansas Division, District of Arkansas, District of West Louisiana, Trans-Mississippi Department (April-September 1864)

1st (Roane's) Arkansas Brigade, 1st (Churchill's) Arkansas Division, 2nd Corps, Trans-Mississippi Department (September 1864-May 1865)

**Battles:**  Helena (July 4, 1863)
Little Rock (September 10, 1863)
Red River Campaign (March-May 1864)
Jenkins' Ferry (April 30, 1864)

## 166. ARKANSAS 37TH INFANTRY REGIMENT

*Also Known As:* Arkansas 29th Infantry Regiment (originally)
Arkansas 1st Trans-Mississippi Infantry Regiment

*Organization:* Organized by companies in March through June 1862. Regiment organized on June 6, 1862. Surrendered by General E. Kirby Smith, commanding the Trans-Mississippi Department, on May 26, 1865.

*First Commander:* J. C. Pleasants (Colonel)

*Field Officers:* Samuel S. Bell (Major, Colonel)
T. H. Blacknail (Major)
John A. Geoghegan (Major, Lieutenant Colonel)
Jeptha C. Johnson (Lieutenant Colonel)

*Assignments:* Fagan's Brigade, Hindman's Division, Trans-Mississippi Department (January-February 1863)
Fagan's Brigade, Price's Division, District of Arkansas, Trans-Mississippi Department (April-November 1863)
Fagan's-Hawthorn's Brigade, District of Arkansas, Trans-Mississippi Department (January-April 1864)
Hawthorn's Brigade, Arkansas Division, District of Arkansas, Trans-Mississippi Department (April 1864)
4th (Hawthorn's) Arkansas Brigade, 1st (Churchill's) Arkansas Division, 2nd Corps, Trans-Mississippi Department (April 1864-May 1865)

*Battles:* Prairie Grove (December 7, 1862)
Helena (July 4, 1863)
Little Rock (September 10, 1863)
Jenkins' Ferry (April 30, 1864)

## 167. ARKANSAS 38TH INFANTRY REGIMENT

*Organization:* Organized by companies in July and August 1862. Regiment organized on September 21, 1862. Surrendered by General E. Kirby Smith, commanding the Trans-Mississippi Department, on May 26, 1865.

*First Commander:* Robert G. Shaver (Colonel)

*Field Officers:* William C. Adams (Lieutenant Colonel)
Milton D. Baber (Major, Lieutenant Colonel)
R. R. Henry (Major)

*Assignments:* Shaver's Brigade, Hindman's Division Trans-Mississippi Department (January-February 1863)
Tappan's Brigade, Price's Division, District of Arkansas, Trans-Mississippi Department (April-November 1863)
Drayton's Brigade, Price's Division, District of Arkansas, Trans-Mississippi Department (January-March 1864)

Tappan's Brigade, Arkansas Division, District of Arkansas, Trans-Mississippi
Department (March-April 1864)
Tappan's Brigade, Arkansas Division, Detachment from District of Arkansas,
District of West Louisiana, Trans-Mississippi Department (April 1864)
Tappan's Brigade, Arkansas Division, District of Arkansas, District of West
Louisiana, Trans-Mississippi Department (April-September 1864)
3rd (Tappan's) Arkansas Brigade, 1st (Churchill's) Arkansas Division, 2nd
Corps, Trans-Mississippi Department (September 1864-May 1865)

**Battles:**  Little Rock (September 10, 1863)
Red River Campaign (March-May 1864)
Jenkins' Ferry (April 30, 1864)

## 168.  ARKANSAS 39TH INFANTRY REGIMENT

*See:* ARKANSAS 30TH INFANTRY REGIMENT, ARKANSAS JOHNSON'S-
HAWTHORN'S-COCKE'S INFANTRY REGIMENT

## 169.  ARKANSAS 45TH INFANTRY REGIMENT MILITIA

**Organization:**  Mustered in with seven companies "to suppress a secret organization opposed to the war" in Searcy County on November 26, 1861.
Mustered out on December 20, 1861.

**First Commander:**  Samuel Leslie (Colonel)

## 170.  ARKANSAS 45TH INFANTRY REGIMENT MOUNTED

**Organization:**  Organized in late 1864. Surrendered by Brigadier General M.
Jeff. Thompson, commanding the Army of the Northern Sub-district of Arkansas, District of Alabama and West Louisiana, Trans-Mississippi Department,
on May 11, 1865.

**First Commander:**  Milton D. Baber (Colonel)

**Field Officer:**  J. W. Clark (Lieutenant Colonel)

**Assignments:**  McCray's Brigade, Fagan's Cavalry Division, District of Arkan-
sas, Trans-Mississippi Department (August-September 1864)
McCray's Brigade, Fagan's Cavalry Division, Army of Missouri, Trans-Missis-
sippi Department, (September-December 1864)
McCray's Brigade, Northern Sub-District of Arkansas, District of Arkansas,
Trans-Mississippi Department (April 1865)
McCray's Brigade, Northern Sub-District of Arkansas, District of Arkansas and
West Louisiana, Trans-Mississippi Department (April-May 1865)

**Battles:**  Price's Missouri Raid (September-October 1864)
Mine Creek (October 25, 1864)

## 171. ARKANSAS 46TH INFANTRY REGIMENT MOUNTED

*Organization:* Organized in late 1864. Surrendered by Brigadier General M. Jeff. Thompson, commanding the Army of the Northern Sub-district of Arkansas, District of Alabama and West Louisiana, Trans-Mississippi Department, on May 11, 1865.

*First Commander:* W. O. Coleman (Colonel)

*Assignments:* Unattached, Shelby's Cavalry Division, District of Arkansas, Trans-Mississippi Department (August-September 1864)

Unattached, Shelby's Cavalry Division, Army of Missouri, Trans-Mississippi Department (September-December 1864)

Northern Sub-district of Arkansas, District of Arkansas, Trans-Mississippi Department (April 1865)

Northern Sub-district of Arkansas, District of Arkansas and West Louisiana, Trans-Mississippi Department (April-May 1865)

*Battle:* Price's Missouri Raid (September-October 1864)

## 172. ARKANSAS 47TH INFANTRY REGIMENT MOUNTED

*Organization:* Organized in late 1864. Surrendered by Brigadier General M. Jeff. Thompson, commanding the Army of the Northern Sub-district of Arkansas, District of Alabama and West Louisiana, Trans-Mississippi Department, on May 11, 1865.

*First Commander:* Lee Crandall (Colonel)

*Assignments:* McCray's Brigade, Fagan's Cavalry Division, District of Arkansas, Trans-Mississippi Department, (August-September 1864)

McCray's Brigade, Fagan's Cavalry Division, Army of Missouri, Trans-Mississippi Department (September-December 1865)

McCray's Brigade, Northern Sub-District of Arkansas, District of Arkansas, Trans-Mississippi Department (April 1865)

McCray's Brigade, Northern Sub-District of Arkansas, District of Arkansas and West Louisiana, Trans-Mississippi Department (April-May 1865)

*Battles:* Price's Missouri Raid (September-October 1864)

Mine Creek (October 25, 1864)

## 173. ARKANSAS 50TH INFANTRY REGIMENT MILITIA

*Organization:* Mustered in with eight companies on March 7, 1862. Mustered out on March 9, 1862.

## 174. ARKANSAS 51ST INFANTRY REGIMENT MILITIA

*Organization:* Mustered in with five companies on March 4, 1862. Mustered out on March 14, 1862.

*First Commander:* J. B. Latham (Colonel)

## 175. ARKANSAS 58TH INFANTRY REGIMENT MILITIA

*Organization:* Mustered in with five companies on February 22, 1862. Mustered out on March 21, 1862.
*First Commander:* J. M. Council (Colonel)

## 176. ARKANSAS 62ND INFANTRY REGIMENT MILITIA

*Organization:* Mustered in with five companies on February 22, 1862. Mustered out on March 21, 1862.
*First Commander:* R. P. Johnson (Colonel)

## 177. ARKANSAS ADAMS' INFANTRY BATTALION

*Organization:* Organized with an uncertain number of companies. Consolidated with Hughes' Infantry Battalion and one independent company and designated as the 23rd Infantry Regiment on April 25, 1863.
*First Commander:* Charles W. Adams (Major)
*Assignment:* Maury's Brigade, Jones' Division, Army of the West, Department #2 (April 1862)

## 178. ARKANSAS BORLAND'S INFANTRY REGIMENT

*Organization:* Mustered in with three infantry companies and one artillery company for the expedition to Fort Smith on April 20, 1861. Disbanded on April 30, 1861.
*First Commander:* Solon Borland (Colonel)
*Battle:* Siezure of Fort Smith (April 23, 1861)

## 179. ARKANSAS BRIDGE'S INFANTRY BATTALION SHARPSHOOTERS

*Organization:* Organized with an unknown number of companies. Consolidated with the 1st (Brooks'-Stirman's) Cavalry Battalion and designated as Stirman's Sharpshooters Regiment on August 1, 1862. Soon broken up. Unclear whether this battalion was reformed.
*First Commander:* Henry W. Bridges (Major)
*Assignment:* Ferguson's Provisional Command, 2nd Military District, Department of Mississippi and East Louisiana (April 1863)
*Battle:* Greenville Expedition (April 25, 1863)

## 180. ARKANSAS CRAWFORD'S INFANTRY BATTALION

*Organization:* Organized with two companies in the spring of 1862. Mustered in for three years or the war on June 23, 1862. Much of the battalion surrendered at Arkansas Post on January 11, 1863. Uncaptured portion was consolidated, as Company A, with those uncaptured portions of the 19th (Dawson's) and 24th Infantry Regiments at Arkansas Post and designated as Dawson's Hardy's Infantry Regiment Consolidated in early 1863. Balance of the battalion paroled and declared exchanged in late 1863. This portion merged into the 8th and 19th (Dawson's) Infantry Regiments in November 1863.

**First Commander:**   William A. Crawford (Lieutenant Colonel)

**Assignment:**   Dunnington's Brigade, Churchill's Division, District of Arkansas, Trans-Mississippi Department (January 1863).

**Battle:**   Arkansas Post (January 4-11, 1863)


## 181.   ARKANSAS (DAWSON'S-HARDY'S) INFANTRY REGIMENT CONSOLIDATED

**Organization:**   Organized by the consolidation in early 1863 of portions of the 19th (Dawson's) and 24th Infantry Regiments and Crawford's Infantry Battalion not captured at Arkansas Post on January 11, 1863. Field consolidated with the 30th Infantry Regiment from March 1864 to mid-1864. Consolidated with the 15th and 20th Infantry Regiments and designated as the 3rd Infantry Regiment Consolidated on November 29, 1864. There is some evidence that this consolidation occured at some time prior to September 30, 1864.

**First Commander:**   Charles L. Dawson (Colonel)

**Field Officers:**   William R. Hardy (Lieutenant Colonel, Colonel)
Francis H. Wood (Major, Lieutenant Colonel)

**Assignments:**   Unattached, Frost's Division, Defenses of Lower Arkansas, Trans-Mississippi Department (May-June 1863)
Drayton's Brigade, Price's Division, District of Arkansas, Trans-Mississippi Department (November 1863)
Tappan's Brigade, Price's Division, District of Arkansas, Trans-Mississippi Department (January-March 1864)
Tappan's Brigade, Arkansas (Churchill's) Division, District of Arkansas, Trans-Mississippi Department (March-April 1864)
Tappan's Brigade, Arkansas (Churchill's) Division, Detachment from District of Arkansas, District of West Louisiana, Trans-Mississippi Department (April 1864)
Tappan's Brigade, Arkansas (Churchill's) Division, District of Arkansas, Trans-Mississippi Department (April-September 1864)
3rd (Tappan's) Arkansas Brigade, 1st (Churchill's) Arkansas Division, 2nd Corps, Trans-Mississippi Department (September-November 1864)

**Battles:**   Red River Campaign (March-May 1864)
Jenkins' Ferry (April 30, 1864)

## 182.  ARKANSAS (HUGHES') INFANTRY

**Organization:**  Organized with an uncertain number of companies. Not separately listed at the National Archives. Does not appear in the *Official Records*. Consolidated with Adams' Infantry Battalion and Adair's Infantry Company and designated as the 23rd Infantry Regiment on April 25, 1862.
**First Commander:**  Simon P. Hughes (Major)
**Assignment:**  Maury's Brigade, Jones' Division, Army of the West, Department #2 (April 1862)

## 183.  ARKANSAS (JOHNSON'S-HAWTHORN'S-COCKE'S) INFANTRY REGIMENT

*Also Known As:*  Arkansas 6th Trans-Mississippi Infantry Regiment
Arkansas 39th Infantry Regiment
**Organization:**  Organized by companies in June and July 1862. Regiment organized in the summer of 1862. Reorganzied by the consolidation of the original companies and the addition of three companies of Gipson's Mounted Rifles Battalion on December 16, 1862. Surrendered by General E. Kirby Smith, commanding the Trans-Mississippi Department, on May 26, 1865.
**First Commander:**  Alfred W. Johnson (Colonel)
**Field Officers:**  John B. Cocke (Colonel)
Alexander T. Hawthorn (Colonel)
Cadwallader Polk (Lieutenant Colonel)
D. W. Ringo (Lieutenant Colonel)
**Assignments:**  Fagan's Brigade, Hindman's Division, Trans-Mississippi Department (January-February 1863)
Fagan's Brigade, Price's Division, District of Arkansas, Trans-Mississippi Department (April-November 1863)
Fagan's-Hawthorn's Brigade, District of Arkansas, Trans-Mississippi Department (January-April 1864)
Hawthorn's Brigade, Arkansas Division, District of Arkansas, Trans-Mississippi Department (April 1864)
4th (Hawthorn's) Arkansas Brigade, 1st (Churchill's) Arkansas Division, 2nd Corps, Trans-Mississippi Department (September 1864-May 1865)
**Battles:**  Helena (July 4, 1863)
Little Rock (September 10, 1863)
Jenkins' Ferry (April 30, 1864)

## 184.  ARKANSAS MCCRAY'S INFANTRY BATTALION

**Organization:**  Organized with nine companies on January 25, 1862. Increased to a regiment and designated as the 31st Infantry Regiment on May 27, 1862.
**First Commander:**  Thomas H. McCray (Major, Lieutenant Colonel)

*Assignments:* Unattached, Trans-Mississippi District, Department #2 (April 1862)
Hogg's Brigade, McCown's Division, Army of the West, Department #2 (April-May 1862)
*Battle:* Corinth Campaign (April-June 1862)

## 185. ARKANSAS MORGAN'S INFANTRY BATTALION

*Organization:* Organized with nine companies between May and July 1862. Mustered in by companies between May and July 1862. Increased to a regiment and designated as the 26th Infantry Regiment on July 23, 1862.
*First Commander:* Asa S. Morgan (Lieutenant Colonel)

## 186. ARKANSAS (PEEL'S-FITZWILLIAMS'-ADAMS') INFANTRY REGIMENT

*Organization:* Organized with only four identified companies in August or September 1862. Disbanded in early 1863.
*First Commander:* Samuel W. Peel (Colonel, Lieutenant Colonel)
*Field Officers:* Charles W. Adams (Colonel)
Hill (Major)
James H. Williams (Colonel, Lieutenant Colonel)
*Assignment:* Cabell's Brigade, Shoup's Division, Trans-Mississippi Department (December 1862-January 1863)
*Battle:* Prairie Grove (December 7, 1862)

## 187. ARKANSAS PETTUS' INFANTRY BATTALION STATE TROOPS

*Organization:* Organized with an undetermined number of companies in early 1864. Apparently mounted in early 1864.
*First Commander:* Allen T. Pettus (Lieutenant Colonel)
*Assignment:* Cabell's Brigade, Fagan's Cavalry Division, District of Arkansas, Trans-Mississippi Department (April 1864)
*Battle:* Marks' Mill (April 25, 1864)

## 188. ARKANSAS STIRMAN'S 1ST INFANTRY REGIMENT SHARPSHOOTERS

*Organization:* Organized by the consolidation of Bridges' Sharpshooters Battalion and the 1st (Brooks'-Stirman's) Cavalry Battalion on August 1, 1862. Soon broken up and cavalry battalion reformed. Unclear whether the sharpshooters battalion was reorganized or merged into the cavalry battalion.
*First Commander:* Ras. Stirman (Colonel)
*Field Officers:* Lafayette Boone (Major)

Henry W. Bridges (Lieutenant Colonel)
**Assignment:** Phifer's Brigade, Maury's Division, Army of the West, Department #2 (August-September 1862)
**Battle:** Grand Gulf (April 29, 1863)
**Further Reading:** McColom, Albert O., *The War-time Letters of Albert O. McCollom.*

## 189.  ARKANSAS TRADER'S INFANTRY BATTALION STATE TROOPS

**Organization:** Organized with an undetermined number of companies in early 1864. Apparently mounted in early 1864.
**First Commander:** William H. Trader (Lieutenant Colonel)
**Assignment:** Cabbell's Brigade, Fagan's Cavalry Division, District of Arkansas, Trans-Mississippi Department (April 1864)
**Battle:** Poison Springs (April 20, 1864)

## 190.  ARKANSAS WILLIAMSON'S INFANTRY BATTALION

**Organization:** Organized with eight companies from the 15th Infantry Regiment Militia ca. March 1862. Reorganized on May 8, 1862. Companies A and B became Companies 2nd I and K, 21st (McCrae's) Infantry Regiment, on May 12, 1862. Battalion disbanded. Company G became Company K, 31st Infantry, Companies C and D became Companies G and F, 1st (Brooks') Cavalry Battalion, respectively, and Companies E, F and H became Companies 2nd E, K and I, 3rd Cavalry Regiment, respectively, on May 25, 1862.
**First Commander:** John L. Williamson (Lieutenant Colonel)
**Field Officers:** D. F. Armstrong (Major)
E. M. Roach (Major)
Milos W. Steele (Major)
**Assignment:** Roane's Brigade, Jones' Division, Army of the West, Department #2 (April-May 1862)

# BIBLIOGRAPHY

Amman, William. *Personnel of the Civil War*, 2 volumes. New York: Thomas Yoseloff, 1961. Provides valuable information on local unit designations, general officers' assignments and organizational data on geographical commands.

Boatner, Mark Mayo III. *The Civil War Dictionary*. New York: David McKay Company, 1959. Provides thumbnail sketches of leaders, battles, campaigns, events and units.

Bowman, John S. *The Civil War Almanac*. New York: Facts On File, 1982. Basically a chronology; it is valuable for its 130 biographical sketches, many of them military personalities.

Daniel, Larry J. *Cannoneers in Gray: The Field Artillery of the Army of Tennessee, 1861-1865*. University, Ala.: University of Alabama Press, 1984. An excellent study of the artillery in the western theater.

Evans, Clement A., ed. *Confederate Military History*. 13 volumes. Atlanta: Confederate Publishing Company, 1899. Each volume of this series primarily provides the histories of one or two states. Each state military account was written by a different participant in the war, and they vary greatly in quality. All accounts, however, include biographies of the generals from their state. The lack of a comprehensive index is the major drawback of this work. Volume XI includes the Florida chapter by Colonel J. J. Dickison. Volume X includes the Arkansas chapter by Colonel John M. Harrell.

Florida Board of State Institutions. *Soldiers of Florida in the Seminole Indian, Civil, and Spanish-American Wars*. Tallahassee: Democratic Book and Job Print, 1903. Provides some background on Florida's Confederate units.

Freeman, Douglas Southall. *Lee's Lieutenants: A Study in Command*. 3 volumes. New York: Charles Scribner's Sons, 1941-1946. The premier narrative study of the organizational and command structure of the Army of Northern Virginia.

―――. *R. E. Lee: A Biography*. 4 volumes. New York: Charles Scribner's Sons, 1934-1935. Also provides organizational information on the Army of Northern Virginia.

Johnson, Robert Underwood, and Buel, Clarence Clough, eds. *Battle and Leaders of the Civil War*. 4 volumes. New York: The Century Company, 1887. Reprinted 1956. Exceptionally valuable for its tables of organization for major engagements.

Krick, Robert K. *Lee's Colonels: A Biographical Register of the Field Officers of the Army of Northern Virginia*, 2nd edition. Dayton, Ohio: Press of Morningside Bookstore, 1984. Brief but very informative sketches of the 1,965 field-grade officers who at one time or another served with the Army of Northern Virginia but never achieved the rank of brigadier general. The second edition also includes a listing by name and unit of those field-grade officers who never served with Lee.

Long, E. B., and Barbara. *The Civil War Day by Day: An Almanac 1861-1865*. Garden City, N.Y.: Doubleday, 1971. An excellent chronology of the conflict, with much information on the organizational changes command assignments.

Lonn, Ella. *Foreigners in the Confederacy*. Chapel Hill: University of North Carolina, 1940. Accounts of the foreign-born contribution to the Confederacy.

National Archives, Record Group 109. Microfilm compilation of the service records of every known Confederate soldier, organized by unit. The caption cards and record-of-events cards at the beginning of each unit provide much valuable information on the units' organizational history.

Scharf, J. Thomas. *History of the Confederate States Navy: From Its Organization to the Surrender of Its Last Vessels*. Albany: Joseph McDonough, 1887. A rather disjointed narrative that provides some insight into operations along the southern coast and on the inland waterways. Unfortunately, it lacks an adequate index.

Sifakis, Stewart. *Who Was Who in the Civil War*. New York: Facts On File, 1988.
———. *Who Was Who in the Confederacy*. New York: Facts On File, 1989. Together, both works include biographies of over 1,000 participants who served the South during the Civil War. The military entries include much information on regiments and higher commands.

U.S. Navy Department. *Official Records of the Union and Confederate Navies in the War of the Rebellion*. 31 volumes. Washington: Government Printing Office, 1894-1927. Provides much valuable information on the coastal and riverine operations of the Civil War.

U.S. War Department. *The War of the Rebellion: A Compilation of the Official Records of the Union and Confederate Armies*. 70 volumes in 128 books divided into four series, plus atlas. Washington: Government Printing Office, 1881-1901. While difficult to use, this set provides a gold mine of information. Organized by campaigns in specified geographic regions, the volumes are divided into postaction reports and correspondence. The information contained in the hundreds of organizational tables proved invaluable for my purposes.

Wakelyn, Jon L. *Biographical Dictionary of the Confederacy*. Westport, Conn.: Greenwood Press, 1977. Short biographies of 651 leaders of the Confederacy. However, the selection criteria among the military leaders are somewhat haphazard.

Warner, Ezra J. *Generals in Gray: Lives of the Confederate Commanders*. Baton Rouge: Louisiana State University Press, 1959. Sketches of the 425 Southern generals. Good coverage of pre- and postwar careers. The wartime portion of the entries leaves something to be desired.

Wright, Marcus J. *General Officers of the Confederate Army*. New York: Neale Publishing Col., 1911. Long the definitive work on the Confederate command structure, it was superseded by Ezra J. Warner's work.

# PERIODICALS

*Civil War Times Illustrated*, its predecessor *Civil War Times*, *American History Illustrated* and *Civil War History*. In addition, the *Southern Historical Society Papers* (47 vols., 1876-1930) are a gold mine of information on Confederate units and leaders.

# ARKANSAS BATTLE INDEX

References are to record numbers, not page numbers.

# ARKANSAS NAME INDEX

References are to record numbers, not page numbers.

# FLORIDA BATTLE INDEX

References are to record numbers, not page numbers.

# FLORIDA NAME INDEX

References are to record numbers, not page numbers.

STEWART SIFAKIS, a free-lance writer on American historical topics, has been a Civil War enthusiast since childhood. He was a student of history and politics at George Washington University and the American College in Paris. Sifakis is the author of *Who Was Who in the Civil War* (Facts On File) and a longtime member of the Civil War Round Table of New York. Originally from Kew Gardens, New York, Sifakis currently resides in Zermatt, Switzerland.